The Weekly Leader

The Weekly Leader

52 Reflections for Becoming a Stronger Leader,
One Week at a Time

Chad Hall

**The Weekly Leader:
52 Reflections for Becoming a Stronger Leader,
One Week at a Time**

For more information, please contact
StrongLead, LLC
407 2nd Street NW
Hickory, NC 28601
admin@stronglead.org

ISBN-13: 979-8864017586
Printed in the United States

To our StrongLead clients and all leaders who sacrifice to make
your corner of the world more like it should be.
Our team admires and respects you tremendously.

~

A special thanks to my daughter, Sydney Hall,
for her kind and helpful work proofreading,
editing, and clarifying this book for publication.

Chad Hall, November 2023

Table of Contents

Introduction

"Leaders live by choice, not by accident" - Mark Gorman

"A good leader motivates, doesn't mislead, doesn't exploit." Proverbs 16:10, "The Message" translation

Let's start simple. What is a leader?

You probably have many pictures come to mind when you hear this question. Perhaps you think about the boss with the big corner office. Or, if you're a sports fan, maybe you think about the best player on the team or the loudest voice in the huddle. You might think of military and political leaders, inventors and pioneers, or legends from days of old. Leadership is a broad concept that can mean different things to different people.

At StrongLead, we care deeply about leadership. We work every day to help leaders grow in their ability to lead others well. As we often say on our podcast, we believe strong leadership is not only about growing your business. It's also about reducing your stress and making life better for everyone around you.

Leaders have the unique ability to influence the future. At its core, leadership involves envisioning a different kind of future and motivating others to take action. Without leadership, nothing would ever change. In fact, you could argue that the world would quickly deteriorate without quality leaders.

On the other hand, imagine a world where strong leadership was the norm rather than the exception. Picture a scenario where people cared deeply about working for meaningful causes and improving their communities. Let your mind's eye see businesses, churches, schools, and even entire nations led by solid, strong, good men and women. Wouldn't you like to live in this kind of world?

This is the cause that drives us at StrongLead to do what we do each and every day. We want Catawba Valley to be a community known for its leadership. We believe that when the leader improves, it causes a cascading effect that also impacts his or her team, organization, family, and community. If we can play a part in developing strong leaders in our community, we feel it will have a positive impact on everyone who lives here.

However, we also know that strong leadership doesn't happen accidentally. Leadership is like a muscle. If you're going to develop your leadership abilities and grow into a stronger leader, it will require some work. It won't always be comfortable or convenient, but if you truly believe in the cause for which you're working, it's worth the added effort.

This premise is the heart behind the book you're holding in your hands (or reading on your screen). We've created a tool that you can work through, one week at a time, over the course of a full year to level up your leadership. In the weeks ahead, we'll address relevant leadership topics ranging from vulnerability, priorities, imposter syndrome, making decisions, giving and receiving feedback, and more. Each entry includes application questions that will help you immediately lock in what you're learning in a way that produces instant results.

These entries are based on our StrongLead podcast, which you can subscribe to on Apple or Spotify to access new episodes each week. You can work through each exercise alone or with your team. You'll find value either way, but there's something especially beneficial about working through this content with others. We've written these exercises to appeal to leaders across all levels within a company. You don't have to have a leadership title to apply the concepts in this book.

Before you get started, take a minute to imagine the best version of yourself as a leader. What do you see? How would you impact your organization? How would you manage your direct reports or interact with your team members? How would you make decisions? How would you uphold your company's core values? How would you train and empower others? Each of these questions reflects an important responsibility within leadership, and this book will help you grow in each of these areas so that you can contribute something truly amazing to the world.

Ready to become a stronger leader? Great! Thanks for joining us, and let's get started.

Week One: Leadership from the Inside Out

Great leaders lead from the inside out. The character and values inside the leader get lived out. When you live and lead from the inside out, it means there's authenticity and integrity behind how people see you leading. It's a far better approach than leadership from the outside in, where you try to be someone you aren't.

If you're going to be an inside-out leader, there are four levels of leadership you want to consider:

Level One: Your core
Leadership starts at a personal level. It starts by being worthy of trust. When you think about yourself at your core, you must evaluate what it will take to become trustworthy. This isn't yet about expecting or commanding trust from others, but it's about determining whether or not you're a person who's worthy of others' trust. What's your personal character like? Do you do the right thing even when others aren't looking? This is the first step of the leadership journey.

Remember that good character doesn't happen accidentally. It takes work for all of us, but it's attainable for everyone. To be an inside-out leader, you must learn to act from strength and do the right thing when it counts, even when there's a substantial cost, or nobody is looking. Character gets developed when you face difficulty and move forward in the face of challenge. Challenge after challenge, through both victory and defeat, your character is formed into that of a trustworthy person.

What values, attributes, or qualities do you possess that make you a person worthy of others' trust?

Level Two: The interpersonal level

As you form relationships with others, the key goal is building trust between you and others. The best relationships are built on trust, and you won't accomplish much unless you can develop trust with others.

As you think about your current relationships, consider whether or not your relationships contain enough trust to withstand the strain they may experience. Like a bridge that can only handle so much traffic, relationships can only handle so much stress. Developing trust can allow relationships to withstand more stress. Remember that before you can lead or manage anybody, you must develop trust with others. Also, don't forget that trust is slowly gained but quickly lost, and we should never take trust for granted.

How much trust exists between you and the team you work with? How could you build even more trust?

Level Three: The managerial level
Once you reach level three, your primary goal becomes empowerment. You've been given power, but what will you do with it?

Weak leaders use their power to rule over others. Their primary objective is to gain more power. However, strong leaders care about using power to help their team reach new levels. By utilizing your power to advance the team, you don't diminish your own power. Rather, you share it by empowering others for a purpose.

Don't be fooled - this doesn't make your work easier. You're not passing off tasks to others because you don't want to do them yourself. You are doing the hard work of developing your team, which is one of the key tasks for any leader.

Who are you currently developing or empowering within your organization? What impact does that relationship have?

Level Four: The organizational level
The target here is alignment. The temptation is to make things about you, but you shouldn't be the focus. Instead, you are aligning everyone around your organization's purpose or mission. Make sure your approach isn't too hands-off or primarily driven by ego. Your job is to keep the mission clear and the culture healthy. You should be willing to step in and lead when things aren't aligned properly while also taking adequate ownership of the problem.

How aligned is your organization? What steps could you take to improve alignment?

Regardless of your role within your organization, it's important to start at the first level and work your way up. Each of us has work to do at our core. Start by becoming a person worthy of trust and continue by thinking about how you can develop greater trust with others.

For more about leading from the inside out, listen to Episode 156 of the StrongLead podcast.

Week Two: Three Lions Every Leader Must Tame

Imagine a lion tamer in a cage with a lion. Although they are standing next to a magnificent beast that could rip them apart, they are able to motivate or encourage the lion to work with them rather than against them.

As a leader, you may not stand in a physical cage and face actual lions, but you'll still need to learn how to subdue and tame various threats that you'll face on a regular basis. Addressing each of these lions requires a proactive mindset defined by the belief that you have the ability to choose your response despite what's happening in the world around you. Remember that this choice is like a muscle - the more you exercise and train it, the more it will grow.

Let's take a look at three specific lions every leader must learn how to tame.

Lion One: Your emotions
Emotions are a necessary part of life. They can even be good at times. However, when they are untamed, they can become a problem. Negative emotions may produce a desire within us to

fight, flee, or freeze when things become challenging. None of these responses are helpful, so we must determine how to control our emotions before they start controlling us.

You won't tame an emotion by getting rid of it. Instead, you must learn how to name your feelings so that they begin to lose control over you. From there, you must exercise your ability to choose how to respond. When you approach your emotions this way, you're not ignoring them, but you're engaging with them in a constructive way.

How are your emotions holding you back? How can naming these emotions enable you to take control over your response?

Lion Two: Your tongue
In the New Testament of the Bible, the book of James teaches that our tongues are like fires that can burn down an entire forest. The author's point was that our words have power, and this power can be used to construct or tear down. Leaders tame their tongues so that their words can have a powerful and beneficial impact. It's not about simply being quiet - it's about making wise choices about what we'll say based on the sort of outcome or impact we desire.

Where could your words have the greatest positive impact right now?

Lion Three: Your focus
As a leader, you're in charge of deciding where you put your time and energy. Your focus will naturally wander to the tasks that require the least amount of energy. You don't have to let your focus bounce around just because it's your natural inclination. To tame this lion, you should identify your priorities

to clarify what's important to you and set up limits to help contain your focus. For example, I have a client who has declared family as his number one priority, and he leaves his mobile phone in his car when he arrives home each day after work. He doesn't retrieve the phone until after his young children are put to bed. If you can clarify priorities and set limits, you'll live a more fulfilling life, and you'll bring incredible value to your work, family, and community.

How is your focus helping you right now? How is it hurting you?

When you tame these lions, they turn into workhorses. All of a sudden, your emotions, tongue, and focus will be allies that help you accomplish what is most important to you.

For more about the lions leaders must tame, listen to Episode 142 of the StrongLead podcast.

Week Three: Are Your Values Out of Whack?

We all have beliefs or principles that guide our behavior. Sometimes referred to as values, these personal principles can include family, innovation, courage, justice, and other important qualities.

It's possible for our values to get out of whack. When this happens, our values lead us astray rather than drive us forward. Proverbs 14:12 says, "There is a way that appears to be right, but in the end it leads to death." We must make sure our values are working for us and not against us.

How can our values serve us well? I'm glad you asked. Here are four ideas to help you ensure that your values contribute positively to your success and personal growth.

Idea One: Perform an honest values audit.
We struggle to admit our values when we think they are unpopular or unconventional. Part of being honest with ourselves (and others) is admitting what we feel truly matters. For example, entrepreneurs who value security may struggle to be honest because they assume all entrepreneurs value risk or

innovation. Rather than aligning our values with others' perceived expectations, we must give ourselves permission to be honest about what we value.

What's a value that you're often not transparent about because you're worried about what others might think? How would your life be different if you were honest about that value?

Idea Two: Distinguish between your real values and aspirational values

Sometimes, we claim values because we feel like they should be important to us, even if they aren't truly our top concerns. You might feel like integrity should be a top value, but you don't actually prioritize integrity above other values. These are aspirational values, whereas lived values are the values we implement or practice in our daily lives.

While holding to aspirational values can lead us to feel better about ourselves, we need to release these aspirational values to determine what's truly most important to us. Give yourself permission to let it go. You don't have to treat it like it's not important, but you should allow it to fall into its true place on your list of values.

What's an aspirational value that you can (or should) release?

Idea Three: Prioritize your values properly

If you take a look at a list of 50 values, you might agree that they are all worth something. However, they also wouldn't each have equal value to you. You should figure out how to prioritize your list of values.

In leadership workshops I facilitate, I give participants a deck of 70 cards, each with a value and a description of that value. I ask them to sort the values into three categories: not important, important, and very important. Even among the values they identify as "very important," most people will have first- and second-order values. This is because a person can highly value only so much.

Your first-order values are ones you will live out no matter what. These are the highest-order values that you hold most deeply. Your second-order values are the values that matter but not to the same degree as your first-order values. Since values can sometimes conflict, you should know what values will win out in times of tension or confusion.

What are 3-4 first-order values and 3-4 second-order values for you? What would happen if a first-order value and a second-order value came into conflict with each other?

Idea Four: Connect your values to actions and results
Talking about values may sometimes feel overly theoretical. Go beyond the conceptual and locate your values in the actions you take and the results you experience. Consider what your values look like in everyday life, and imagine what your life would look like if you aligned your days and your responsibilities around your highest-order values.

How do your first-order values connect with everyday actions and results?

As a leader, you must first lead yourself. If you are living outside your values, there is a breakdown in your leadership of self. We all have this kind of breakdown to some degree. This is why evaluating how your values are working for you and how they align with your everyday pursuits is so worthwhile. It will help you live a life of greater fulfillment, abundance, and impact. Allow your values to work for you rather than stumbling into a situation where you are a slave to your values.

For more about making sure your values are working for you, listen to Episode 157 of the StrongLead podcast.

Week Four: Leaders Bring Vision

As leaders, we often talk about vision, but we don't always fully understand what vision actually is. If you spend enough time in leadership, you'll quickly realize that vision is highly important yet not enough. There's a biblical proverb that says, "Where there is no vision, the people perish." (Prov. 29:18 KJV)

Disaster comes when vision is absent because without a vision, there is no direction, no coordination, no cooperation, and no forward movement. The alternative is chaos and stagnation leading to death.

Since vision is so crucial, let's look at four questions that you must answer as you determine your vision and evaluate how to bring vision to your team.

One: What is vision?
Vision is about seeing a preferred future and being able to communicate it with others so they can see – and actively participate – in the pursuit of that vision. Obviously, you can't fully predict the future, but you can imagine a preferred future or

the way things could be, and you can share it with others so they can see it as well. In other words, vision is the ultimate reality of what you're aiming for and why it matters.

What do you want the future to look like? Try to think several years into the future. How does this ideal reality inform your company's vision?

Two: What makes vision important?

You can't create something if you don't know your role. When others can see the vision, they understand the part they play, and they can contribute to making the vision a reality. Your vision dictates your priorities, coordinates your efforts, and helps you determine what to do – and what not to do. Without a vision, it's easy to get lost in politics, personal agendas, and petty disagreements. Vision aligns team in a way that's motivating.

What impact does your vision have on your team? How could you strengthen that impact?

Three: How do you bring vision?

Start by imagining things as you want them to be. This isn't a natural skill for every leader, so don't be discouraged if you have to spend a few weeks or months thinking this over. Regardless of how much effort it takes, it's worth the effort. Remember that you need a centralized vision and not several visions. Once you have a picture of what you want the future to look like, think about how you can craft your communication in a clear and compelling way. You'll need to do this repeatedly in everyday interactions because vision leaks. You should also look for ways to connect your vision to the everyday work your team does.

What's most compelling about your vision? How could you impact others when they hear you communicate your vision?

Four: Why is vision not enough?
Vision is crucial, but you can't lead with only vision. If you think in three layers, vision is the highest level. Strategy is the next layer down, and below strategy, you find tactics. For your vision to have an impact, it must be backed up by strategy and tactics. You must know the plan for bringing your vision about, and you must understand how your daily actions will help you pursue your vision day in and day out.

How do your strategy and your tactics connect back to your vision? What would strengthen this connection?

If you're the leader, vision is a keystone responsibility that supports and enables everything else you're doing. It's worthwhile to get clear about what your vision is and how you could do a better job of communicating that vision. Most of the time, you don't need a new vision – you just need to improve at communicating the vision you already have. This can have a tremendous impact on your team and your organization.

For more about bringing vision to your team, listen to Episode 89 of the StrongLead podcast.

Week Five: How to Be Effective

You can be busy without being effective. Sometimes, the busier we feel, the less effective we are. Effectiveness doesn't always come naturally, but it's something we can all learn. Let's consider five ways you can be more effective in life and leadership.

One: Focus on time

To be effective, you have to make the most of your time. Everyone has the same amount of time, but by paying attention to how you spend it, you can make the most of every minute you have. Consider tracking your time so you know what you're spending your time working on. This will allow you to evaluate whether or not your time is going to the highest good. Ultimately, you'll be able to leverage your time by planning in advance how you'll spend it.

On a scale of one to ten, how effectively are you spending your time? What will it take to raise your grade?

Two: Focus on contributions

What contribution is required of you? Being effective starts with knowing what impact you're trying to have. At home, it might be being the best spouse and parent you can be. At work, it could mean defining your individual contribution. Whatever that contribution is, think about whether you have the time and the ability to fulfill that contribution well. If you're lacking in skills or competencies, it's your responsibility to grow in your capabilities so you can meet expectations.

What's the key contribution required of you at work? What will it take for you to make the best possible contribution?

Three: Focus on strengths

If you spend the majority of your time working to bring your weaknesses up to match your strengths, you'll have a hard time rising above mediocrity. You're better off making your strengths so strong that your weaknesses are irrelevant. You can't ignore all your weaknesses, but your time and energy are better spent working in your areas of key strength. Take time to define your strengths, acknowledge your weaknesses, and focus your attention on your strengths.

What are your 2-3 core strengths? How could you spend more time working on these areas of strength and further developing them?

Four: Concentrate

You'll always have more ideas than you will time to execute them. You must be able to prioritize your ideas and put the first things first. You have to understand what's important to you and block out distractions. You can do this on a high level by defining goals for certain months and seasons, and you can do it on a smaller scale by thinking through what your most important tasks are each day.

What's most important right now, based on the season you and your company are in? How can you do a better job of focusing on your priorities?

Five: Decisions

Effective people make high-leverage decisions that eliminate the need to make future decisions. It's possible to make one high-leverage decision that compounds into future decisions. For example, if you can decide what your core values are, it makes many future decisions faster and easier. You won't have to work as hard to decide who to hire and what you'll expect from your team members. Another high-leverage decision is understanding what type of business you're in.

What's one decision you could make that would eliminate the need to make future decisions?

If you're not striving to be effective, you're wasting precious time and energy. There are people around you who are counting on you to be effective. As you think about these five areas, pick one to focus on initially. You can incorporate the others over time, but starting with one will make it easier to follow through.

For more about being effective in life and leadership, listen to Episode 87 of the StrongLead podcast.

Week Six: Five Kinds of Power

What exactly does it mean to empower someone? We talk about this concept often, but it's easy to get confused about what this actually means. Let's try to shed some practical light on what it means to empower someone so we can understand how to do it and do it well.

When you empower someone at work, you're giving them power (or making sure they have the power) to make decisions and take action. Empowerment and delegation aren't the same thing: delegation is a little more limited, whereas empowering is much more broad.

If we wanted to get a little more specific, we could say there are five kinds of power we give people when empowering:

One: The authority
Authority can be formal or informal. Formal authority often comes from a title or position, but informal authority usually shows up during times of crisis. This goes beyond what the organizational chart says and has more to do with how you've "cleared the path" ahead of them so people know you've given

them authority.   It's your job to provide informal authority.
Only with both kinds of authority can a person you've
empowered really take action and make decisions.

*Think about someone at work who you want to empower. How could you
"clear the path" for them so that they can exercise authority?*

Two: The ability

If you're going to empower someone, it's your job to make sure
they have the skills, knowledge, and traits necessary to do the
job. If they don't have the skills yet, you don't have to be the one
to do the training, but you're in charge of making sure they have
the training or can get the training. It's not enough to tell an
employee to figure it out on their own.

*If you're going to empower someone to serve in a certain capacity at work,
what skills or abilities do they need to possess? What kind of training or
coaching could help them grow in that area?*

Three: The confidence

Confidence acts as the dimmer switch on people's abilities.
Maybe they have the skills necessary to perform a task, but if
they don't believe they can do it, that ability won't come out.
You can't force confidence upon people, but you can support
them in growing their confidence by assuring them that you're
confident in them and listening for areas where they are already
confident.

*What are some other ways you can support employees to develop greater
confidence?*

Four: The resources

We often take for granted the resources we have, which can lead us to ignore the fact that others don't have those resources. If the other person is going to get the job done, they need access to the proper resources. This could include access to the company credit card, a particular department, or a team of people to help. You don't have to provide unlimited resources, but don't withhold resources that are necessary for getting the job done.

What resources do you use on a regular basis to do your work? Which of these resources would you need to share if you're going to empower someone else?

Five: The power of vision

To empower others, you must help them see the "why" behind what you're trying to do. If they don't see the full picture, they won't be able to bring their best. Sharing the vision will provide the context needed to get the job done well.

What's your company's overarching vision? How does sharing this vision play a role in empowering others?

If you're being empowered, make sure you have the proper amount of power in each of the above areas in order to do the job well. If you're the one empowering others, use this as a checklist that drives conversations with the team members you're empowering. Talk with them through the list and be open to their feedback if they don't feel like they have all the power they need.

For more about how to effectively empower others, listen to Episode 165 of the StrongLead podcast.

Week Seven: Four Rules for Challenging

Do you like being challenged? The answer is probably both "yes" and "no." In one sense, we like the idea of doing difficult things. At the same time, many of us prefer the comfort and convenience of living without challenge.

If you aspire to be a leader, you must become accustomed to challenging situations. Moreover, good leaders know how to challenge others in a way that helps them continually grow and achieve their potential. When you approach challenges this way, you find opportunities to elevate yourself and the people around you.

So, how do you challenge the right way? Here are four rules that apply in all situations regardless of your role or rank in your organization.

Rule One: Receive more than you give
Before you can challenge others, you must be willing to receive challenge yourself. This means accepting constructive feedback and embracing difficult conversations without deflecting blame or becoming defensive. By modeling this approach, you're

providing an example of what it looks like to be on the receiving end. Even if you don't agree with every challenge that comes your way, you are showing others that it's OK to be challenged.

How well do you receive challenges? How could you better model or embody what it looks like to receive challenges well?

Rule Two: Challenges must serve your vision

While it's true that challenge can be beneficial, it's not true that all challenge is created equally. For a challenge to serve a greater purpose, it must connect back to your organization's vision. Since challenges and changes are uncomfortable, your fellow team members must understand why they matter and what greater purpose they serve. As German philosopher Friedrich Nietzsche once said, "He who has a why to live for can bear almost any how."

How can you better fulfill your organization's vision by effectively challenging your team members?

Rule Three: Be specific but not personal

A challenge should not be a personal attack. It's not about ego or character. At the same time, you want the challenge to be specific so that the recipient can clearly understand what standard is expected of them. For example, if you're challenging a team member who is making sloppy or careless mistakes, be specific about what you're seeing and what gap your team member must fill to take their game to the next level. At the same time, while you're doing this, you're making the challenge about performance and behavior (and not about personality or any innate traits).

Think about a time when you received a specific challenge. How did it help you grow or improve?

Rule Four: Frame challenge as a guard against the spread of weakness

Weakness is like a virus or cancer, and challenges are a guard against that weakness. If you leave weaknesses unattended, they will spread. Strength doesn't work this way. Imagine if you only ever lifted ten-pound dumbbells. After a while, not only would you stop growing stronger, you'd actually start to get weaker. In the same way, if you don't increase your challenge over time, weakness will begin to spread throughout your organization. Gradually increase your level of challenge, and your team's strength will continue to grow and develop.

Think about 1-2 areas where you would like to see your organization grow stronger. How could challenge help you develop in these areas?

It's natural to feel uncomfortable when you experience challenges. However, we must remember that struggle leads to growth. If you can learn how to embrace discomfort and leverage challenges as opportunities, you'll unlock new levels of potential within yourself and your organization.

For more about effectively challenging, listen to Episode 162 of the StrongLead podcast.

Week Eight: Why Is Urgency So Appealing?

On a scale of one to ten, how close do you think you are to fulfilling your potential?

Many organizations don't realize their potential because they are distracted by matters that are urgent but not important. Urgent tasks are constantly crying out, "Hey, this must be done right now, and you need to do it." While important tasks help us fulfill our goals or pursue our vision, urgent tasks are more tempting in the short term.

Thankfully, we can overcome the allure of urgency by recognizing what contributes to its appeal. Let's look at three reasons why urgency can be so tempting.

Reason One: Completing urgent tasks offers immediate gratification
As human beings, we are hardwired for immediate gratification. Our brains prefer activities that offer instantaneous rewards. Generally, we would rather stay quickly stuck than move forward slowly. We stay quickly stuck when lots of effort and activity gets us nowhere meaningful. Even though progress can only be

measured over time, we don't look up to see if we're moving forward. We may be in motion, but that doesn't mean we're headed in the right direction.

For example, many leaders would rather do something themselves than empower others. While this offers immediate results (getting the job done), it doesn't allow you to train and develop your team members. As you think about your approach to work and whether you're focusing more on urgent or important tasks, consider investing your time in a better long-term outcome rather than simply spending time on getting things done.

In what ways are you currently investing your time? What are 1-2 additional ways that you could improve yourself or your organization by sacrificing short-term gratification for a better long-term result?

Reason Two: Urgent tasks don't require as much effort
When we prioritize what's urgent, we aren't making any decisions about what to focus on. We are simply reacting to the circumstances and situations around us. Highly productive work happens when there is a distance between the decision and the action. The closer the action is to the decision, the less productive your work tends to be. There should be a separation between your decisions and actions, and ideally, you'll be the one doing both. While this is hard work, it's also highly productive.

What decisions can you make today about how you will direct your focus that will make you more productive in the future?

Reason Three: Prioritizing urgency prevents us from disappointing people

It's easy for all of us to fall susceptible to the desire to please people. Saying no is hard (and we usually try to avoid hard things). However, as a leader, you must develop the skill of saying "no." Showing empathy and being generally agreeable isn't a bad thing. However, you can easily get pulled away from your top priorities if you don't know how to say "no." Remember, as a leader, you're not called to go with the flow. You're called to BE the flow.

What are 2-3 tasks that you need to say "no" to, even if saying "no" will cause some momentary disappointment?

As you can see, urgency is a major temptation for many people. However, keep in mind that nobody is forcing you to do anything. You have control over how you spend your time, and if you learn how to spot the temptation of urgency, you can take steps to avoid drifting off course.

For more about the temptation of urgency, listen to Episode 161 of the StrongLead podcast.

Week Nine: Be Vulnerable the Right Way

How comfortable are you showing vulnerability at work?

Vulnerability is the kryptonite for many otherwise strong leaders. Too many leaders don't know how to be vulnerable the right way. Some leaders shy away from vulnerability, while others overdo vulnerability in the pursuit of affirmation or validation.

Effective vulnerability isn't about oversharing or unpacking all your emotional baggage. It's about looking at yourself objectively and being willing to notice the good, bad, and ugly within yourself. If you can take an honest look at your own strengths and weaknesses and be willing to share what you see with your team, you'll be a better leader and team player.

Whether you're brand new on your team or have been leading your organization for several decades, you'll benefit from embracing vulnerability. Let's think about four steps that will help you better engage with vulnerability.

Step One: You must have the humility to grow.

Humility is an accurate assessment of yourself in the order of things. When we talk about vulnerability, humility shows up as our ability and our willingness to see ourselves objectively. Humility says, "I am not what I can be yet, but I have the potential to be more." Even if you feel like you're at the top already, you must recognize that you can still reach another level. This requires vulnerability and humility but also provides an opportunity for growth.

On a scale of one to ten, how would you assess your humility? How could you raise your score by 1-2 points?

Step Two: You must be eager for feedback.

Leadership guru Ken Blanchard once said, "Feedback is the breakfast of champions." Feedback helps us spot our blind spots and learn specific ways we can get better. Even if we don't agree with the feedback, we must process the content as we consider the source. Receiving feedback with eagerness – and even asking for constructive feedback – requires a high level of vulnerability.

How well do you receive feedback? How often do you solicit constructive feedback from others?

Step Three: You must become more comfortable with being wrong.

Not every decision you make will work out perfectly. Not every idea you have will be valuable or worthwhile. Everyone is wrong sometimes. When we don't get it right, we must remember it's not about us. We shouldn't feel inadequate when we're wrong, but we also must be willing to admit when we're wrong rather than seeing ourselves as perfect or infallible. The strongest leaders, the ones who are truly worth following, are the ones who are ready and willing to admit when they were wrong. If you are able to do this, your team will be able to deal with it and move on.

Think about a time when you were wrong. What was your response? How could you have handled it better?

Step Four: You must be excellent at collaboration.
This step is different from the first three, but that doesn't make it any less important. If you can learn how to hear others' ideas and allow them to provide feedback on your own ideas, you will supercharge your leadership. Collaborative leaders don't care about who gets the credit. They are eager to validate others and hear what they have to say.

How often do you work with others on projects or key initiatives? What additional opportunities for collaboration come to mind?

Weak leaders are too insecure to admit their mistakes, acknowledge room for improvement, and collaborate with others when working on key goals and objectives. Don't allow your insecurities to limit your influence. Be courageous enough to see yourself objectively and share your perspective with your team. The people around you will appreciate your honesty, and you'll discover new levels of success within your leadership.

For more about being vulnerable the right way, listen to Episode 159 of the StrongLead podcast.

Week Ten: Running the Plays You Call

A football team must follow a few distinct steps to run a play properly. First, the coach must design the play. Secondly, when the time is right, they have to call the play. Finally, although it may seem obvious, the members of team must run the play. Each step is essential, and the play won't be effective unless all three steps are followed.

In some ways, this is a metaphor for life and business. It's common for individuals, families, and organizations to take time away from the day-to-day to pull away and assess their current state. They may decide to make some adjustments, but when they get back in the game, nothing changes. They make great plans, but they don't execute once the whistle blows.

It's one thing to design and call a play, but it's another to actually run it. You can call great plays but struggle to gain traction because you're not executing your plans. This can not only keep you from creating positive change, but it can even cause you to lose traction or progress.

Most teams achieve good results when they follow through on the ideas and strategies they work hard to develop. There's a chance that the only thing keeping you from a higher level of success or impact is the ability to execute the plans you design. It's easy to stop following the playbook when you become impatient or feel like you aren't seeing results as quickly as you would like. We must be willing to continue to execute our plans.

Simply put, plays that work will work, but only if we decide to run the plays. We can say that something is a priority, but nothing will ever be different if we don't commit to acting on the priority. You may not run the plan perfectly the first time, and that's OK. Continue to run the play, knowing you will improve your execution over time.

Here are four quick tips to improve your execution:
1. **Up the clarity**. Vague ideas always lose to clear plans. Design concrete steps to clarify how you will execute your approach.
2. **Clear the path**. Remove any barriers that could prevent you from carrying out your plans.
3. **Create accountability**. If you commit to running a play, check back in to track your team's progress and see how things are going.
4. **Leverage your strengths**. It's hard to decide to do something that you don't have the talent, strength, or knowledge to do effectively. You'll have an easier time running plays that feel natural for you and your team.

As we wrap up, remember that executing the plays you call does not mean that you have to stick with a bad plan. A football team may have different plays in their playbook, but they all aim to get the ball in the end zone. It's OK to recognize that your plan needs to be changed to raise your chances of reaching your goals. However, make sure you are properly running whatever plays you design and call.

Here are a few questions to consider as you process this material:
1. What are the go-to plays in your playbook?
2. How effectively are you running these plays?
3. If you could commit to better executing the plays you call, what would the result be for yourself, your family, and your team?

For more about running the plays you call, listen to Episode 158 of the StrongLead podcast.

Week 11: Four Relationship Moves

Relationships are an essential part of each person's life. Few things have a greater impact on us than the people who we surround ourselves with. Some people push us to be better and bring out the best in us, while others may knock us off track or drain us of energy. How can we make the most of our relationships?

Most people have around 50 key relationships that have a direct impact on their quality of life. Take a minute to do an audit of your most important relationships. You may not see these people daily, but interactions with them mean something to you. They can be family members, friends, coworkers, or others you know in your community.

Once you have that list, think about how much each person contributes to your life and your well-being. It's not about whether you like the person but about how they push you toward your purpose and the best version of yourself. This will help you see who has a strong positive influence on you and who isn't impacting or helping you as much.

Obviously, if someone is having a negative impact on your life, that relationship will need some sort of change. Don't pass off ownership for making this change to the other person. Instead, assume that the other person won't change and take up the responsibility for yourself for setting the relationship on a different course.

In addition, each person must make four moves to receive the greatest return or value from the relationships in their life. These moves won't require anything from the other person - they are each within your wheelhouse:

1. **Attitude moves.** You can improve a relationship simply by changing your attitude or expectations. In turn, this will diminish the negative impact of the relationship on your well-being. This doesn't mean we withhold timely and constructive feedback, but it does help us think about how we can impact the situation by shifting our perspective.

2. **Boundary moves.** While you can't ask people to change their beliefs or values, you can be clear about what they can do to or with you. Do your relationships have clear boundaries? Are you able to communicate and reinforce these boundaries?

3. **Communication moves.** Speaking of communication, how do you communicate with other people? Your relationships could be improved by more clear, assertive, or vulnerable communication. Perhaps your relationships aren't what you want them to be because you're not communicating your expectations or needs.

4. **Delete moves.** Typically, this isn't your only option or your first option. At the same time, sometimes

decreasing the time you spend with one person is the best option if you realize that someone holds you back or brings out the worst in you.

Improving our relationships isn't only about keeping ourselves happy. It's also about creating a life with more purpose and meaning, as well as cultivating situations where we can grow and become the best versions of ourselves. As we make these relationship moves, we will prepare ourselves to have a more significant influence and impact on our organizations and our local communities.

Application questions
1. What relationships could benefit from one of the above moves? Try to come up with two or three relationships that could improve.
2. On the other end of the spectrum, think about 3-4 relationships that benefit you in a positive way. How can you show appreciation to these people, and how could you invest more time or energy in these relationships?

For more about making relationship moves, listen to Episode 155 of the StrongLead podcast.

Week 12: How Do You Work Best?

What are the unique ways that you contribute to your workplace, family, church, volunteer organization, or community?

This question is important for us to make sure we have the proper tools for the job at hand. You wouldn't want to show up to work on a project with a hammer when a chainsaw is what's needed. Too often we assume we are the right tool for any job, but no one has what it takes for all the different situations and circumstances that can arise. As a singular human being, you have certain skills and traits that make you distinct from other people. You must develop the self-awareness necessary to figure out how you do your best work. Knowing what you bring to the table will enable you to make a more significant impact as a leader.

There are three different angles to consider as we evaluate how we best work. Let's dig into each one.

Question One: When are you most productive?
Some people love working early in the morning before
distractions start presenting themselves. Others prefer to work
late and burn the midnight oil. Whether you're an early bird or a
night owl, you'll do better work if you can determine what time
of day you're at your best.

This is especially important for knowledge workers. If a big part
of your job involves creating content or solving problems, you'll
benefit from doing this work during your ideal time of day.
You'll naturally have more energy, and you'll tackle problems
more effectively.

Question Two: With whom do you do your best work?
Some people do their best work alone. They prefer to be in
complete control of their projects and their schedule. Others
find that they are most productive when there's some degree of
collaboration involved. This could mean that they identify as
part of a team, or they might simply stay in touch with a
teammate or a supervisor through regular check-ins.

Not all jobs allow you to choose your ideal option, and that's
fine. Regardless, it's still important to know yourself, your
preferences, and your tendencies. If all things are equal, when do
you do your best work? Once you know the answer to this
question, you can adjust your work environment to set yourself
up for success and ensure you get the right amount of
collaboration with others. You may also share your perception
with your supervisor to see if they can help you create a situation
where you're more engaged or productive.

Question Three: What is your best energy rhythm?
Some people do their best work in short bursts of energy with
lots of variety. There's another type of person who wants to
focus a little more but will still work on several tasks in one day.
Others do their best work when they have a small number of
focuses each day, and, of course, there's also the person who
wants to focus on one thing for several days. Wherever you fall
on this spectrum, knowing your energy rhythm will help you
gravitate toward whatever routine helps facilitate your most
productive work.

Each question on this list requires you to understand yourself
and how you're uniquely wired. Rather than going with the flow
or doing what others are doing, you must make adjustments
based on what you know about how you can bring your best. As
we wrap up, consider one or two adjustments you can make to
do more of your best work.

*For more about learning how you work your best, listen to Episode 154 of
the StrongLead podcast.*

Week 13: Overcoming Imposter Syndrome

There's a disease that inflicts millions of leaders each year. It's not high blood pressure, COVID, or hemorrhoids. Honestly, it may be more serious than any of those examples.

Countless leaders struggling with imposter syndrome. These leaders don't feel they are worthy of their positions or their accomplishments. If you're dealing with imposter syndrome, you may tell yourself that you're only experiencing success because you're lucky or because you stumbled into favorable circumstances. You may feel pressure to prove yourself to others in addition to yourself in order to confirm that you belong.

If you experience imposter syndrome but don't deal with it, you may still experience some level of success. However, you won't come close to reaching your potential, and you won't be able to enjoy or appreciate any of the accomplishments you are currently experiencing. Perhaps most notably, you won't be able to share your success in a way that lets others benefit and participate without tension.

Sometimes, imposter syndrome comes across as a false sense of humility. However, it seems as though many people who are experiencing imposter syndrome truly feel inadequate to some degree. They could be driven by perfectionism and a fear that someone would notice their flaws. Other leaders are naturally skilled and intelligent, but they look around and feel like they aren't where they should be. They know they bring some value to the table, but they question why they haven't experienced the success they think they merit or deserve.

Leaders struggling with imposter syndrome may wear these disguises as well:

- **The expert.** These leaders don't feel like they belong, so they work hard to learn as much as possible from books, podcasts, and seminars. They feel like they must know everything in order not to be perceived as a fraud.
- **The solo pilot.** This person believes that they aren't adequate or qualified if they have to ask for help. They are committed to flying solo even if they crash the plane.
- **The superhero.** This leader takes on more tasks than they can handle to prove how capable they are. The world needs to be saved – and it's up to them to do the saving!

You can't fix imposter syndrome with simple tips or tricks. Instead, you must take a more substantial approach. Here are a few ideas:

- **Offer yourself courageous compassion.** Look at yourself in the mirror. Be honest about how you're feeling. Don't try to talk yourself out of what's going on - just pay attention to what's there.

- **Take a dose of humility.** Selfishness fuels imposter syndrome. Dealing with imposter syndrome requires admitting that life isn't all about you. Leadership isn't about feeling good - it's about doing good for someone besides yourself.
- **Find your worth elsewhere.** Your leadership and your work will never give you total fulfillment. Value and worth cannot be earned. You must find your intrinsic value in something besides your accomplishments or your competence.

As you process this material, try to relax and release the temptation to measure yourself against your own expectations. Instead, compare yourself to who you were yesterday and celebrate the improvements you're making. Growth always requires work, but it's also a process that brings out the best in you.

Application questions
1. Have you struggled with imposter syndrome before? What was that experience like?
2. What approach or idea for dealing with imposter syndrome most resonates with you? Which do you find most challenging?
3. Where else can you find your sense of worth or value besides your work?

For more about overcoming imposter syndrome, listen to Episode 153 of the StrongLead podcast.

Week 14: Generosity and Leadership

Stinginess never leads to success. Many people think they must be a manipulator in order to get ahead in life. This narrow way of seeing the world comes from a scarcity mindset and the limiting belief that there aren't enough resources to go around.

The truth is that most things in life are abundant. There's plenty to go around. If you learn how to live with an abundance mindset, you'll begin to see the world as a place that is always generating new resources for others. Not only is there enough for everyone, but there's also an innate capacity to make more.

There are four specific areas where you can be generous at work and in life, and lucky for you, they all start with the letter "t."

One: Be generous with your time
The concept of being generous with time is one of the most important principles to get right. If we can't be generous with our time, we'll struggle to be generous with much else.

Being generous with your time does not mean that you must give all your time away. Instead, it often looks like sharing time with other people to address their needs and concerns. You may not receive anything in return for your time, but you are choosing to be generous and serve another person's interests.

How can you be generous with your time? What people or situations could benefit from you sharing your time?

Two: Be generous with your talent
You likely have some skills, knowledge, and abilities that others don't possess. Instead of using those gifts to only benefit yourself, you can be generous and use your strengths to help others. Keep in mind that sharing your talent may also involve sharing your time, which reinforces generosity with time as the basis for each other topic we'll discuss here.

How can you be generous with your talent? What talent (or talents) might you choose to share?

Three: Be generous with our treasure
Your mind may immediately go to money when you read this heading, but your treasure goes beyond your financial resources. For example, being generous with your treasure means you are willing to lend your power washer or your lawnmower to your neighbor who's in need.

When you do this, you have to keep your expectations low for what you'll receive in return. You understand that it could create work or inconvenience for you down the road, but all generosity comes with inherent risk because you don't know it will be received. At the same time, generosity isn't about the return you receive from giving. Instead, it's about meeting others' needs with the resources you have.

How can you be generous with your treasure? Where do you have excess or margin that you could use to serve others?

Four: Be generous with your talk
A person with a stingy mentality avoids praising people too much because they don't feel like it contributes to their own image or portrayal. On the other hand, someone with a generous mentality is quick to share words of affirmation with others. This posture requires us to be generous with both our time and our status.

Who in your life could benefit from receiving some generous "talk?"

One final question exists. Why is it important to be generous? First of all, generosity is not about adding additional value for you as the person being generous. Rather, generosity simply makes the world a better place. Not only will it benefit the people around you, but it will contribute to your own growth and development.

For more about generosity and leadership, listen to Episode 150 of the StrongLead podcast.

Week 15: Three Habits for Every Leader

Have you ever noticed that great leaders don't seem like they are working that hard to lead? Obviously, there's a lot taking place behind the scenes that we don't always see, but there's also this sense that leadership comes easily or naturally to them.

Part of the reason why this is the case is that many leaders make doing the right thing automatic through the development of strong habits. When you have great habits, you don't have to put forth as much effort to make good things happen.

While there are many habits that you can adopt and develop, there are three specific habits that will help you reach a higher level as a leader. If you can make these three behaviors habits, leadership will require less effort and become more easy or natural.

Habit One: Intentional meetings
Many people hear the word "meeting" and immediately feel frustration or dissatisfaction. However, meetings are the best aspect of work for many leaders who view these times as opportunities to influence others and achieve a desired outcome.

These leaders make sure each meeting has a purpose and is conducted in the right way.

To establish this habit, here are two questions you can ask:
1. What needs to happen?
2. What meetings do I need to have in order to make that happen?

If you can answer these two questions, you'll define a purpose for each meeting, and you will do your part to make sure meetings are achieving (or progressing toward) the desired goal. If you're attending a meeting that you didn't call, you can still practice this habit by beginning the meeting with a question such as, "What do we hope to accomplish during our time together?"

Habit Two: Curious listening
Leaders are adept at listening first. In the words of 7 Habits pf Highly Effective People author Stephen Covey, leaders must seek first to understand and then to be understood themselves. The trigger for this habit is often a disagreement or conflict. A poor leader will jump in early to state their case and push their way forward. A great leader will listen first to understand the other person's perspective, and they will reflect this understanding even as they explain their side.

Habit Three: Clear decisions, clear directions
A great leader can end conversations with clear takeaways and action steps. A conversation is only productive if it produces something. Leaders make sure conversations are productive in that they lead somewhere and end with a clear decision or action

step. Leaders can also connect the "big picture" vision with the specific conversation at hand to clear up any confusion or ambiguity.

As we wrap up, consider how strong each habit is for you. On a scale of one to ten, how would you rate your competence in each category? From there, think about what would help you grow in each area. How can you bring intentionality to your growth? Who can help you grow this habit? Working in these areas will help you become the best leader you can be.

For more about essential leadership habits, listen to Episode 98 of the StrongLead podcast.

Week 16: Do You Have the Right Stuff?

Perhaps you've read Tom Wolfe's book "The Right Stuff" or seen the movie based on Wolfe's book. "The Right Stuff" is about the early astronaut program and the first test pilots. In this book, Wolfe explores the courage and other innate qualities these first astronauts possessed and how they became successful.

In business and in life, the right people are the ones who have the "right stuff" to get the job done. Your job may not be orbiting the earth or breaking the sound barrier, but you still must possess certain qualities and traits in order to be an influential leader. Let's take a look at four specific attributes that effective leaders must bring to the table.

Quality One: Humility

To be humble is to have an accurate assessment of yourself in the natural order of things. You're not placing yourself higher than you should, but you're also not devaluing or demeaning yourself. In work, humility matters because of how it impacts your approach to your work. Rather than thinking the job is here to serve you, you can recognize that you're called to serve through your job.

How would you evaluate your current level of humility? How would those closest to you describe your humility?

Quality Two: Drive

Drive is the ambition or the motivation to achieve. It pairs well with humility because humility alone can diminish drive while drive alone can lead to an overemphasis on self and personal gain. When you can bring the right amount of drive and humility to the table, you'll create incredible opportunities for yourself.

How driven are you? How does your natural drive work alongside your current level of humility?

Quality Three: Growth mindset

A growth mindset contrasts with a fixed mindset. A fixed mindset accepts things as they are and rejects the responsibility or the desire to change. On the other hand, a growth mindset sees opportunities to add new skills and develop additional strengths and competencies that don't yet exist. A person with a growth mindset is willing to get better, while somebody with a fixed mindset doesn't see their potential or care about reaching new heights. An eagerness to learn and grow will set you apart from the crowd.

How easy is it for you to identify areas of potential growth? What are 2-3 areas you would like to grow in?

Quality Four: Eager for guidance

This final concept encapsulates the other three. If you don't have drive, humility, or a growth mindset, you won't seek out a mentor, teacher, or coach. Somebody who wants to be a better version of himself will be eager to solicit help from somebody else. If you don't currently have a mentor, look for somebody who's experienced some success and is willing to share their experiences and the lessons they learned along the way. This person shouldn't try to convince you to be just like them, but they should adhere to certain principles and values that underline the work they do.

Who do you know that could make a good mentor or coach for you? Or, if you're further along in your career, you might be a good mentor for someone else. Who could you pour into?

Aiming to have the right stuff has zero downsides. It's not only good for you, but it's good for the people around you. Push yourself to demonstrate each of these qualities and look for a mentor or coach who can help you along the way.

For more about having the right stuff, listen to Episode 148 of the StrongLead podcast.

Week 17: Fear of Making a Decision

You may have heard of FOMO (Fear of Missing Out), but are you familiar with FOMAD? FOMAD is the fear of making a decision, and it is an issue for many leaders, even seasoned and otherwise strong leaders. Some people struggle with making the decisions themselves, while others have a hard time allowing others to make decisions. Many businesses fail as a result of poor decision-making, so it's important to get it right.

Improving decision-making starts with empowering other decision-makers so that more people can be involved in the decision-making process. While it may sound counterintuitive, the best place for decisions to be made is at the place with the least competence. This doesn't mean that you allow incompetent people to make decisions. Instead, you allow competent people to make decisions at the lowest level in the organization rather than unnecessarily elevating decisions up the ladder. For example, a frontline employee in a furniture manufacturing plant can make certain decisions rather than elevate those decisions to their supervisor or the plant manager.

If you're the type of person who suffers from FOMAD, it's important to think about how you can improve your decision-making abilities and become more comfortable with making decisions efficiently. Let's discuss four steps that will help.

Step One: Clarify what decisions you should make
You should embrace your responsibility to make decisions, but you also don't want to overstep your boundaries. Ultimately, you'll feel more confident when you're making the decisions you know are yours to make. If you manage others, be crystal clear about the decisions you want them to make and plan to reinforce this desire over time. If it's your job to make the decisions, be open to the encouragement and feedback you receive from others.

What are the decisions you can and should make? How do you feel about making these decisions?

Step Two: Know your decision-making preferences
Generally, there are two approaches to making decisions. One approach is to think through all the relevant facts: the options, the pros and cons, and the bottom line. The other approach prefers to think about human elements such as relational harmony. The latter approach has more to do with thinking, while the second approach has more to do with feelings.

Do you prefer a thinking- or feeling-oriented approach to making decisions?

Step Three: Integrate the two approaches
Each of us has a preference, but it's essential to integrate both elements to make the best decision possible. Some decisions will naturally involve more thinking elements, while others may be

more oriented around feelings. Regardless, becoming a more effective decision-maker requires you to give attention to both domains as you consider the factors of the decision at hand.

How can you intentionally bring in the other element in a way that helps you make better decisions?

Step Four: Clarify what you know
Clarifying what you know starts with, obviously, stating what you know. However, it also involves recognizing what you can't know as well as what you don't know yet. There's a clear difference between these two categories, and identifying what questions fit into each domain will help you determine how you can move toward clarity when making a decision. This approach reminds you that you will never have all the facts, but it helps you see what answers you must seek out before you can make a well-informed decision.

How would you further define the difference between what you can't know and what you don't know yet? How is that distinction helpful to you?

The world needs more responsible and willing decision-makers. Even if you aren't an owner or a high-ranking leader in your organization, you will stand out if you're able to make good decisions and empower others to decide. Also, remember that decisions factor into everyday life and relationships as much as they come into play at work. Don't back away from making decisions – embrace the opportunity to become stronger through discernment and action.

For more about making decisions, listen to Episode 146 of the StrongLead podcast.

Week 18: Driving Results

Have you ever thought about the difference between someone who is simply filling a position or going through the motions and somebody who is truly contributing? Often, it comes down to the degree to which somebody is driving results. As a reminder, a result is an outcome that you can't directly achieve. Results are different from goals or objectives, where your activity immediately correlates with achievement.

Since results don't happen accidentally, you must work to drive results. How can you do this? Let's take a look at three tips or principles that will help you drive results in your organization, team, family, or community.

Tip One: Connect results, objectives, and activities
You should be able to see how your activities help you meet your objectives, which leads to the results you desire. This result may be your business's profit, the impact you hope to make in the community, or the quality of life you provide to your employees. It's easy for organizations to get lost in the activity and find themselves doing things that don't correlate with their results. As a leader or manager, it's your job to maintain this clear line of sight for yourself and your team members.

Think about your organization's key purpose and top values. What results would connect with the fulfillment of your purpose?

Tip Two: Distinguish busy work from important work
Important work drives results. Once you identify your desired results, you can determine what work will help you achieve these goals. From there, you'll use the Eisenhower matrix, or the distinction between important and urgent work, to consider how you're investing your time in the work that truly matters. You'll have to save time to handle tasks that are both urgent and important, but you can also limit the amount of time you spend on projects or issues that are urgent but unimportant.

Do you spend more time on important or urgent tasks? How can you automate, eliminate, or delegate more of the work that is urgent and unimportant?

Tip Three: Track your activities and your objectives
Perhaps you decide to do an inventory of how you're spending your time to get a better idea of what you're doing throughout the day. When you do this, you may discover you have a surprising amount of slack or margin in your schedule. You could also find that your objectives and the way you spend your time aren't in alignment with each other. If this happens, you may need to reconsider your key objectives or your daily schedule.

If you were to track your time for just one week, what do you think you would learn?

Ultimately, driving results is about working smarter and not harder. It's about considering which activities will produce the highest return on your time. Your organization or business exists for a reason, and the results you produce matter. Be a person who drives results, and you will stand out as a valuable high performer.

For more about driving results, listen to Episode 145 of the StrongLead podcast.

Week 19: What Drains Vision?

As a leader, you're tasked with defining your organization's vision and sharing that vision with others in a compelling manner. It's tempting to think that your work is over after you communicate the vision. However, it's easy for vision to leak over time by powerful forces that can drain vision if we aren't aware they exist. Here are five holes you must plug to protect your vision.

Force One: The whirlwind
You can get lost in the day-to-day operations of your business and forget the reason why you exist. To combat this potential pitfall, you should connect the whirlwind to your vision. Remind your team that the activities in the whirlwind are helping you fulfill your greater purpose. Do this on a regular basis, and not just once in a while.

What are the daily activities your team must do to keep up with the whirlwind? How do these tasks connect to your vision?

Force Two: Lack of progress

Your vision can be far in the future, and it may feel like you're never going to get there, even if you're making small progress. Ultimately, your vision is the accumulation of many goals. The vision becomes clearer as you reach goals, but it's easy to feel discouraged when the progress seems intangible. As a leader, you can help your team celebrate the process even when progress feels out of reach. Remind your team that you're doing the work that will lead to results, even when patience is in short supply.

What process is your team following to reach its goals? How can you celebrate or acknowledge the value of this process?

Force Three: Lack of sacrifice

When people aren't asked to sacrifice for a vision, they will wonder if the vision really matters. They could also struggle to experience the vision is real and tangible. It's natural to feel reluctant to ask people to sacrifice. However, some degree of sacrifice is motivating when you're working with the right people. In addition to asking people to make some sacrifices en route to reaching your vision, you should also model what it looks like to sacrifice yourself.

What are 1-2 sacrifices that may be necessary for your organization to achieve its vision?

Force Four: Drama

Drama in the workplace competes with the story you're attempting to write based on your vision. Drama distracts from the meaningful story and draws people into a story that is less significant and more toxic. It's also a sign that your vision isn't as strong or active as you want. This could be a people problem, but it could also mean that you haven't clearly communicated your vision in a way that's compelling or motivating.

How could your vision guard against the start or spread of drama?

Force Five: Naysayers
A naysayer says, "This can't be done," or "This isn't important." They aren't the people who are asking hard questions to help you clarify or discern ideas. They are the individuals who are bringing a spirit of pessimism and toxicity to your team that distracts from your vision. If you're going to build something great, you have to stop the spread of this type of talk. Similar to calling out drama, this gives you an opportunity to cite the vision as the reason for the standard you have in place.
If you chose not to tolerate the negativity of naysayers, what impact would it have on your organization?

Remember, effective leaders intentionally overcommunicate the vision. It's your job to keep the vision in front of people and fight against potential leaks and drains.

For more about preventing the drain of your vision, listen to Episode 144 of the StrongLead podcast.

Week 20: Five Hard Truths About Leading

It's easy to see leadership romanticized. Pop culture and social media can paint a picture of leaders and leadership that is overly idealistic. As anyone who's been a leader for more than a few days knows, leadership can be incredibly difficult. When you understand what you're getting yourself into as a leader, you're less likely to walk away when times get hard.

Hard Truth One: "Knowing" is easy. "Doing" is hard.
To be honest, knowing isn't always easy either, but it's still nowhere near as difficult as taking action. There's value in learning about leadership and gaining insights from others, but what will separate a truly strong leader from a pretender is the application of what you're learning. Don't be surprised when it's challenging to implement the ideas you discover in this leadership guide, our StrongLead podcast, or anywhere else.

What's the hardest aspect of "doing leadership" right now? What's the value in continuing to work at it?

Hard Truth Two: Leading people is messy.

This likely won't come as a surprise. People are messy, and leading people will always be messy. Everyone has a unique personality, and you may even find that some people don't want to be led (by you or by anyone). You're likely to experience pushback, and you'll discover that what works with one person doesn't work with someone else.

How can you stay energized and motivated even when leading others gets surprisingly messy?

Hard Truth Three: A leadership role is a responsibility, not a reward.

Jesus tells a parable in the Bible about three servants asked to invest their master's fortune. One servant wisely invests what's entrusted to him and is promptly given even more responsibility. This story reminds us that our hard work is often returned with additional work to be done. When you are promoted to a leadership position, it's not a time to relax. Instead, you'll likely have more issues to deal with than before.

How does this perspective on leadership change your approach to managing and empowering people?

Hard Truth Four: Most change initiatives fail

Leaders often have the goal of driving profits, promoting changes, and making things better. According to Harvard Business Review, 70% of change initiatives will eventually fail. The truth is that the pull of the status quo is like the pull of a river's current. Though we may try to change the flow, people will naturally fall back into the way things have always been done. Leaders can feel discouraged or demotivated by this, but strong leaders have a more resilient mentality. They recognize that change is difficult, and they know many initiatives fail because leader gives up too early.

What's an important change initiative you're working on right now? How can you stick with this change even when it becomes difficult?

Hard Truth Five: Leaders create and destroy culture
A healthy, strong culture takes years to develop and only a few weeks to destroy. The higher up you are in your organization, the more responsibility you take for building the culture. If you're in a position with influence and authority, you'll have to spend time and energy on creating an environment that attracts (and retains) top talent.

How would you describe the current culture at work? How are you contributing to making it better?

Some people may wonder why anyone would want to be a leader if it's so hard. The truth is that strong leaders have a clear and compelling purpose that makes the struggle worthwhile. When you have a cause that drives you to get up and go to work each morning, you'll be willing to embrace and overcome these five challenging truths.

For more about these hard leadership truths, listen to Episode 140 of the StrongLead podcast.

Week 21: What Motivates You?

Sometimes, you have a clear vision or purpose but lack the motivation to get started or keep moving. Since motivation is the desire to act in service of a goal, knowing how to develop and maintain motivation is crucial for all leaders. There are three levels of motivation that you must understand if you're going to harness its power and use it to achieve your desired results.

Level One: Survival

If a bear is chasing you, the goal is clear. You want to run away so you don't die.

Level Two: Rewards and punishments

If your survival isn't in question, your motivation may be driven by a desire to get something good or avoid something bad. The good or bad thing may not even be connected to a long-term goal, but it may be an instantaneous outcome. This type of motivation is usually external and reflects the traditional carrot-and-stick mentality you often hear about.

Level Three: Internal motivation

Level Three is the deepest type of motivation, but it doesn't mean that Level One or Level Two motivations don't exist. However, studies show that people are motivated by more than survival, rewards, or punishments. Each person has an inner drive to learn, create, or contribute to something bigger than themselves. This form of motivation is often what drives people to work toward goals or outcomes that truly matter.

If you're going to be successful as an organization, you'll need to learn how to tap into Level Three motivation. The good news is you can train your people (and yourself) to be more intrinsically motivated. It's not an instantaneous decision, but it's something you can work toward over time.

Here are three ways you can increase your own intrinsic motivation as well as the intrinsic motivation of those around you:

- **Autonomy.** Someone with a strong sense of autonomy feels like they are able to lead themselves and make their own decisions. *What are 2-3 specific ways that you could allow your team members more autonomy in their work?*
- **Mastery.** Mastery means you're getting better at something that matters. People want to feel like they are getting better at what they are doing. Sometimes, this requires setting the vision for your team about what mastery looks like for each person. *How can you equip your team to pursue (or identify) mastery?*

- **Purpose.** When you feel like you're contributing to a greater cause, you have a sense of your purpose. *How can you enable your team to define their sense of purpose and connect it to the work they do each day?*

Remember that these three steps aren't binary. Instead, think about them like a scale or spectrum. Each domain can be a part of a person's role to some extent. Look for ways to add additional autonomy, mastery, and purpose to each person's work. Meanwhile, consider how each area intersects with your own work and impacts your own motivation.

For more about what motivates people, listen to Episode 139 of the StrongLead podcast.

Week 22: Three Areas You Need to Balance

How do you find the right balance? It's an important topic for leaders because of how easy it is to get out of balance. Although we often think about balance in a static way, it's important to remember that balance is dynamic. If we're going to maintain balance for the long haul, we must constantly work on maintaining the right amount of balance.

More specifically, there are three key areas you must address as you think about establishing balance. Let's take a look at each one in detail below.

One: Reflection and action
Reflection is when you call a timeout to step back and notice what's happening around you. This doesn't necessarily have to be a vacation or significant time off from work. Instead, it's the regular habit of stepping back to evaluate what's taking place and asking questions such as, "Am I headed in the right direction?" Or, "Am I making progress?" On the other hand, action is the process of taking steps based on what you learn or recognize during your reflection.

As a leader, you can't spend too much time focusing on one area and ignoring another. If you're all about reflection and failing to take action, you'll never make any progress. If you're always acting and never reflecting, you'll quickly grow tired, and you may fail to notice how the situation or landscape is changing around you. If you're going to be successful, you must recognize that both action and reflection have their place.

Is it easier for you to reflect or act? How can you establish a greater degree of balance between reflection and action?

Two: Task and relationship

All endeavors of life involve tasks and relationships. Tasks are directly connected to performance, whereas relationships are more about who you're doing the tasks with. Depending on your content, you may find that one of these domains is more important than the other. However, it doesn't mean that the other area isn't important. Finding balance means giving attention to both tasks and relationships.

In your life, what could it look like to have the right balance between tasks and relationships? How can you take steps toward the ideal situation?

Three: War and peace

Most people prefer peace, but life really does involve both. If you're going to have a great life, you must know when it's time to go to war. Conflict is sometimes necessary, and some hills are worth dying on. A person of convictions is willing to fight for their convictions, and strong leaders are aware of their convictions and willing to stand up for them.

At the same time, you must balance your willingness to go to war with a desire for peace. The purpose of life is not to be in endless war with one another. We engage in conflict in the pursuit of peace, and we desire peace as our default conviction.

What are 2-3 convictions you're willing to fight for? What could it look like for you to go to war to uphold these convictions while still desiring peace in a broader sense?

Be thinking about what the right combinations could look like in your life. Imagine your life over the next twelve months, and think about what it could look like to have balance in each of the above areas. Consider writing these six words down on a notecard and leave it in a place where you will see it often. Let this serve as a reminder of the need to pursue balance in the key areas of your life.

For more about finding balance, listen to Episode 138 of the StrongLead podcast.

Week 23: Three Layers of Delegation

The ability to delegate is like a superpower. If you can effectively delegate, you expand your impact and influence. However, the inability to delegate holds many leaders back from reaching their potential.

As you think about delegating, it's important to remember that delegation does not equate to giving away work. You're not outsourcing the tasks you don't enjoy. Rather, you are getting important work done through other people. Like doing a load of laundry in a washing machine, you're still doing work to get work done even if you aren't directly involved in the completion of a task.

Another topic to consider is what it looks like to delegate in layers. Obviously, you're delegating responsibility, but there's a deeper way you can think about the way you delegate. Let's look at three levels of delegation to consider how you can become better in each area.

Layer One: Goals

Goals are outcomes. You may have a goal for how many items you want to sell or how much profit you want to bring in. Goals can also be less tangible, such as a goal to build a better workplace culture. For the sake of this exercise, imagine you're a restaurant owner with the goal of having a cleaner restaurant.

Layer Two: Plans

Plans are systems that describe how you plan to accomplish goals. If you're the restaurant owner who wants a cleaner dining room or kitchen, your plan could be a schedule detailing how often you'll clean each space and who will be in charge. The plan may also include instructions about how the plan will be communicated to everyone involved.

Layer Three: Actions

Actions serve as individual steps you take as a part of a plan or in pursuit of a goal. Within our restaurant example, action steps could include designing the schedule, assigning certain people to tasks, and holding them accountable to get things done.

There are a few things to keep in mind as we think about each layer. First, even if you're only delegating specific action steps, it's still important to explain the goals and the plan to each person involved. Additionally, you must remember that delegation can be a process. Perhaps you don't delegate the entire action step of designing the schedule the first time, but instead, you create a schedule that your team can use, knowing that they will be able to do it themselves in the future after seeing what you've created.

Lastly, we must recognize that many leaders only ever delegate actions. It's the easiest kind of delegation to do. The problem is that when you make this a habit, your team sits and waits for you to give them something to do. Delegating actions is a great place to start, but it's a terrible place to stop. Try to stretch into the plans (and even the goals) when appropriate so that you can build your team's confidence and competency.

Here are a few questions to consider as we wrap up:
1. On a scale of one to ten, how would you rate your current ability to delegate?
2. When you delegate, are you most often delegating goals, plans, or actions?
3. As you think about the current landscape of your work and your team, what 2-3 opportunities come to mind where you could incorporate additional delegation?

For more about effective delegation, listen to Episode 137 of the StrongLead podcast.

Week 24: The Power of Sacrifice

What comes to mind when you think about sacrifice? There are several possible images that may come to mind. Essentially, sacrifice is a willingness to give up something today for something better tomorrow. There's a degree of risk or uncertainty within the value exchange, but there's a willingness to make the potential investment regardless.

In leadership, there are four sacrifices you must be willing to make. Let's talk about how these sacrifices can lead to invaluable rewards.

Sacrifice One: Pleasure for strength
A key sacrifice is giving up pleasure today for strength tomorrow. This means choosing not to do what is easy or convenient right away in order to do something that isn't quite as enjoyable but will contribute to the development of long-lasting strength. The reality is that if you stay in your comfort zone for too long, you'll begin to wonder why you don't have what you desire. You're hanging onto the easy way (or the way you've always done things), and this is why you aren't experiencing anything different.

Where do you need to sacrifice pleasure for strength? What difference would that sacrifice make?

Sacrifice Two: Ego for meaning

Ego is all about how you feel about yourself. It's the selfish part of who you are. Strong leaders are willing to sacrifice status for significance. Rather than craving the spotlight, you're willing to work toward long-term meaning even when you can't immediately see the results. In the words of former President Harry S. Truman, "It's amazing what you can accomplish when you don't care who receives credit."

If you cared less about getting credit and more about creating meaning, how would you lead differently?

Sacrifice Three: Security for impact

You won't have an impact if you're too invested in holding onto security. There's nothing inherently wrong with security, which is why this is a sacrifice. In the Bible, God calls Abraham to leave his home country. God promises to make Abraham the father of a great nation, and Abraham sacrifices security for the potential to make an impact.

Where could you have a greater impact if you were willing to sacrifice some of your security?

Sacrifice Four: Performance for growth

Leaders place a high emphasis on performance because they want to deliver on the promises they make. However, we must still recognize that performance is connected to what we get done today, while growth is increasing our ability to perform in the future. In other words, you're sacrificing some degree of performance today in order to perform at a higher level tomorrow.

How could you sacrifice a percentage of performance today to achieve a higher level of growth and future performance?

If you want to achieve a higher level of success, it's going to require some sacrifices. Start with imagining what type of success you desire. From there, consider what sacrifices from each domain it will take to get you to where you want to go.

For more about the power of sacrifice, listen to Episode 136 of the StrongLead podcast.

Week 25: Leaders Are Organized

Getting things done is often an uphill battle. The road ahead can be chaotic, and many leaders waste time and energy trying to check off tasks in an inefficient manner. Ultimately, you'll have to establish some level of organization in your life in order to be an effective leader, even if organization is not your natural tendency. Let's talk about four areas of life that must be organized.

One: Your priorities
If you don't know what's important to you, you won't be able to organize anything else. Organizing priorities becomes much easier once you can identify what they are.

In addition to determining what you want to get done, you should also define the areas where you want to develop. It could mean expanding your knowledge, honing additional skills, or designing new processes. Since development is how you grow your capacity to get things done, you'll enhance your ability to do more in the future when you focus on development as a priority.

How clear are your priorities right now? How could you get your priorities more organized?

Two: Your processes

A process is the way you go about doing something in order to achieve a reliable outcome. A checklist is a type of process. So is a written standard operating procedure, a meeting agenda template, or a routine. Smart leaders leverage processes anytime they can, especially for things that come up often and need to be done right.

You want to organize your processes because they support you in getting the right things done well. They act as the catalyst between your priorities and your actions, and they make your actions easier by showing you what you need to do each time a common situation comes up.

What are 1-2 processes that are especially helpful for you? What are 1-2 areas where you could benefit from better defining or establishing an ongoing process?

Three: Your actions

Organizing your actions includes thinking about the focus, time, and energy you spend in order to reach your priorities. Obviously, this will be easier to do when you have helpful processes in place, but there's still some work to do in order to organize your real-time actions in pursuit of a particular goal or outcome.

What are some actions you spend a good percentage of your time on? How could these be better organized?

Four: Your space

Your space is the area around you, including your office and desk. It's also your electronic files such as your Google Drive, Dropbox, or email inbox. Each area needs to be properly organized in order to help you work effectively.

On a scale of one to ten, how would you rate the current organization of your space? How satisfied are you with that rating?

The best tool to organize the first three categories (priorities, processes, and actions) is the Eisenhower Matrix, which was further popularized in Stephen Covey's "Seven Habits of Highly Effective People." Using this tool, you can determine what activities are urgent and/or important.

Remember, when you don't know what's important, you'll naturally gravitate toward tasks that are urgent. However, urgent tasks aren't always important. What's urgent and important will naturally get done, but when you have a chance to choose between working on something that's only important but not urgent and something that's only urgent but not important, importance should always win.

For more about becoming more organized as a leader, listen to Episode 134 of the StrongLead podcast.

Week 26: Why Leadership Matters to a Community

It's easy to understand why leadership matters in a business, school, church, nonprofit organization, or family. Have you ever thought about what makes leadership important in the broader community?

At StrongLead, we care deeply about building the reputation that Catawba Valley is a place where strong leadership exists. We see three reasons why leadership is important in this community, as well as in other places throughout the country and the world.

Reason One: The "snowball" effect
When strong leadership exists at the smaller level, good things happen. Problems are being solved, and gaps are being closed. When leaders become stronger, there's a snowball effect where momentum is built, and more problems are solved. Eventually, you reach a point where life is improving for everyone in the community. Leaders are natural problem-solvers, and not just in the company or organizations where they work.

Where do you see problems being solved and gaps being closed because of the leadership in your local community? What role do you play in this process?

Reason Two: Synergy

Synergy can feel like a made-up word, but it's a real concept. Synergy exists when the whole is greater than the sum of the parts. Synergy can cause 1+1 to equal more than two. The more strong leaders you have in a community, the more you'll see people collaborating. When strength and strengths come together, this creates a powerful synergy that exponentially multiplies influence and impact.

How are you collaborating with other leaders and teams in your area? How does this produce synergy?

Reason Three: Psychological well-being

If the people in your community need rescuing or if they are looking to complain or place blame, it can be a miserable place to live. This type of scenario is all too common in situations where leaders are weak, and it's usually an indication that people don't feel like they have agency. On the other hand, when you look at communities that are flourishing, you see people who feel like they control their life and their circumstances. Strong leaders can build this type of mentality within their communities where people feel like they have ownership. You'll get a lot accomplished, but you'll also notice a heightened sense of self-esteem.

What do you sense the level of agency is within your local community? What might be possible if there was a higher sense of ownership?

Now that you know more about the value of strong leadership within the local community, here are three steps you can take:

1. **Develop yourself.** Don't point fingers and expect others to do the dirty work of leading. Be willing to roll up your sleeves and get to work.
2. **Develop the leaders around you.** Pour into your team, family, and neighbors. Work alongside each person to help them become stronger.
3. **Invest in your community.** If you're in Catawba Valley, we would love for you to partner with our nonprofit, the Catawba Valley Leadership Foundation. Its mission is to develop strong leaders for the benefit of the entire community. Visit our website at catawbaleadership.org to learn more.

Craig Groeschel, the Senior Pastor of Life Church and host of the "Craig Groeschel Leadership Podcast," often says that everyone gets better when the leader gets better. This isn't just true within businesses and organizations but also within communities. Every great community needs strong leadership, and you can play a role in building strong leaders no matter where you live.

For more about leadership in a community, listen to Episode 133 of the StrongLead podcast.

Week 27: The Power of Baby Steps

Everywhere we look, change is needed. However, change can be hard. Oftentimes, you'll have to take baby steps in order to facilitate effective and meaningful change. This is true in your personal life, and it's true at work as well. You won't transform overnight into a new person, but you can make a gradual shift over time by taking small, deliberate steps.

There are many reasons why baby steps are so powerful, but four stand out. These steps are helpful in any area of life where you're looking to create change.

Reason One: Baby steps allow us to learn with small failure
Failure is a great teacher, but it's often easiest to receive in smaller doses. As the old proverb says, "Never test the depth of the water with both feet." Big leaps carry big risks, and while we may idolize people who willingly take massive risks, we often fail to recognize that these big risks were preceded by small failures. Also, keep in mind that small failures can still provide big lessons.

What's a small failure you recently experienced? What did you learn from that failure?

Reason Two: Momentum needs to start somewhere

The energy to get something started is greater than the energy required to keep something moving. Change is similar. Making the first move will help you conserve energy for later in the process. If you try to do everything at first, it can be overwhelming. Think about how you can use some energy to get started while still saving some energy to keep things moving later on. When you think in terms of baby steps, it's easier to imagine what this could look like.

What's a change you've been thinking about making? How can you get this change started with a small step?

Reason Three: Small steps add up

Small steps may not seem significant each time, but they can eventually add up to significant progress or growth. However, this is only true if you're taking small steps in the same direction. Some people constantly do little experiments and wonder why their work isn't compounding. The impact is limited because their actions aren't focused.

What's your primary long-term goal or objective? How can you keep your small steps aligned around this vision?

Reason Four: Baby steps lead to giant strides

Once you build some momentum and confidence, you'll lengthen your strides and start running down the track. The goal of taking baby steps isn't to take baby steps forever. Over time, you'll begin taking larger steps based on the foundation you built from starting small. You wouldn't test the depth of the water with both feet, but you also can't swim unless both feet are in the water. Baby steps are powerful because they lead you to the point where you're ready to hit your stride.

How will you know when you're ready to dive in and start moving forward faster?

As we wrap up, consider where you need to get started by taking baby steps. It could be within your professional life, your family, your health, or somewhere else. What's a change that you need to make, and what's the smallest step that would represent forward momentum? Once you discover what the first step is, be willing to take it even if it's hard. Keep going, and you'll be amazed to see where you end up in a few months or years.

For more about taking baby steps, listen to Episode 132 of the StrongLead podcast.

Week 28: Using Routines to Stay Focused

Focus is hard to come by in today's world, but it's incredibly powerful for anyone who can harness its potential. If you're going to accomplish anything significant, you're going to need to figure out how to leverage the power of your focus.

In many ways, focus is like a muscle. For focus to become stronger, you must stretch and develop it over time. In this entry, we'll cover four specific routines that can help you build greater focus.

One: Routines to end and begin the day
While that arrangement may seem awkward, this particular order is intentional. It's impactful to think about how the intentional ending of one day feeds into the beginning of another. For starters, this routine will help you get better sleep at night. From there, you can work on building the habit of getting up at the same time each day. Eventually, you'll reach a point where you don't need an alarm clock to wake up at the same time each day, and you'll find that you experience fulfilling and productive mornings that feed into great days.

How would you describe your current routines to end and begin the day? How could they be improved?

Two: Routines around growth

The seventh habit of "The Seven Habits of Highly Effective People" is sharpening the saw. Stephen Covey uses the metaphor of a man cutting down a tree repeatedly with the same saw. Over time, the saw will become dull if he doesn't intentionally set aside time to sharpen it and the work of sawing will get more and more difficult as the saw grows duller. The habit of sharpening the saw involves taking time to invest in yourself instead of continually driving performance.

What holds many people back from taking time to sharpen their metaphorical saw is feeling like they don't have time. They don't realize that prioritizing growth and development will make them more effective and productive in the future, thus cutting down the amount of time they need to complete the same work. As we talked about in Week 22, leaders must be willing to sacrifice performance for growth. If we don't have routines to facilitate growth, it probably won't happen. Whether it's establishing habits for worship, learning, or physical activity, these routines will help you keep on track toward the growth you desire.

What growth routines do you currently have? What's one you would like to start?

Three: Routines around planning

Planning is a waste of time if you don't do anything with the plans you make. On the other hand, if you commit to following the plans you develop (or, as we talked about in Week Four, running the plays you call), planning can be one of the most impactful tasks you complete on a regular basis. Routines will help you effectively plan for the future. Consider implementing annual, monthly, weekly, and daily plans for maximum effectiveness.

How do you plan for the future? How helpful are these plans?

Four: Routines around review
It's easy for leaders to focus primarily on the here and now. At the same time, it's essential to prioritize occasional reviews to make sure you're headed in the right direction. It's the same reason why you should occasionally look out the rearview mirror while you're driving as opposed to always looking forward. In addition to identifying potential learning opportunities, the review also enables us to celebrate what's going well.

When will you set aside time to review? What specific activities or time periods will you review?

Routines help us be our best. Specifically, routines help us focus on what matters most. Think about how you can incorporate better routines in your life to build discipline and achieve the progress you desire.

For more about routines that will help you focus, listen to Episode 131 of the StrongLead podcast.

Week 29: Four Numbers to Decrease

You probably have a good idea of the numbers you want to increase. You wouldn't be upset about more profit, sales, or revenue. On the other hand, have you spent time thinking about the numbers you want to go down? Let's take a look at four numbers that should decrease as you level up in leadership.

One: Fewer decisions

This sounds counterintuitive at first. Aren't leaders the ones who make critical decisions? Yes, and as you go up in leadership, you might make fewer decisions overall, but you'll make more higher-leverage decisions. This is important because you never want to experience decision overload or decision fatigue. You want to remain sharp so you can be ready and able to make the most critical decisions. To do this, you'll have to delegate some decisions that don't have to be made by you.

What are 2-3 decisions you have on your plate that you could delegate to someone else? How would that impact your ability to make more important decisions?

Two: Fewer goals

Goals are great, but this doesn't mean you need to have an endless number of goals. If everything is important, nothing is important. More goals don't always equate to more impact. For some, it will help to think in terms of performance goals and development goals. Performance goals usually involve counting metrics and won't require much of your focus. Development goals are more about growth, and as you move up in leadership, these goals deserve the majority of your focus. As you meet these goals, you'll increase performance as a result.

How can you reshape your performance goals into development goals? What would success look like in each of these areas?

Three: Fewer direct reports

When we talk about direct reports, we're talking about the people you manage or supervise. As you go up, the number of people you manage should go down. This matters because you aren't just managing their performance, but you are also pouring into these people and helping them develop. You'll be able to do this more effectively if you don't have an overwhelming number of direct reports.

How many direct reports can you effectively manage and develop while still being able to give proper attention to your own initiatives?

Four: Fewer problem employees

As you move up in leadership, you'll get more of your results from other people. When you reach this level, you can't afford to have people on your team who are problematic. Your team members must be assets and not liabilities, especially if they are in roles that involve supervising or managing. Don't forget that promotions come to problem-solvers, not problem employees.

How can you tell if an employee is a "problem" employee? If this happened, how would you appropriately respond?

At the heart of each of these numbers is your ability, as a leader, to say "no." This takes discipline and commitment, and both of these qualities are critical for strong leaders to have. If you can develop the ability to say "no," you'll effectively say "yes" to pursuing your potential and developing into a tremendous leader.

For more about these four numbers, listen to Episode 130 of the StrongLead podcast.

Week 30: Developing Your Executive Presence

Your presence has to do with how you come across. When others evaluate your presence, they are trying to decide if you are someone worth trusting or following. In the context of leadership, this is incredibly important because your ability to influence people directly correlates with your presence. People will be colder if you have a poor presence, but if you have a strong presence, people will be more likely to follow the path you set.

So, how do you develop a better presence? First of all, let's identify a few things that can damage your presence:

- **Being emotionally reactive.** You don't have to be stoic, but you should avoid strong emotional reactions that are out of proportion with what's happening.
- **Being overly _BOLD_.** Think about when someone's words to you were the equivalent of bold, italicized, and underlined text. That kind of assertiveness is overwhelming, isn't it? Some people will come across this way in an effort to appear especially strong or

confident. It's off-putting and doesn't positively impact your executive presence.

- **Being overly uncertain.** These are the people who don't share ideas because they don't feel like the idea is perfect, or they are always apologizing when they do speak. A high degree of uncertainty is easy to perceive and can give people the wrong impression.

Now that we've identified some killers of executive presence, let's think about how to build a better presence. This boils down to three important characteristics: how you act, how you speak, and how you dress. Those all seem obvious, and they do matter. However, the outside won't get properly addressed until you improve the quality of what's happening on the inside. If you can do the interior work, the exterior work will be easier.

Good executive presence requires accepting yourself despite your flaws. This doesn't mean that you aren't actively looking for ways to improve, but it does mean you're content with factors such as your appearance, your background, and your natural tendencies that you can't control. You know who you are, and you accept yourself.

This self-acceptance leads to a realization that life isn't all about you. If you're not OK with yourself, you'll subconsciously make everything about you because you're trying to fill a void. A good executive cares more about the outcome and the mission than proving himself or herself. When you boil this problem down to its roots, a bad executive presence is usually caused by a lack of ego or too much ego.

From here, you can think about how to improve the exterior elements. You'll act better under pressure because you can keep your composure under fire. You'll be more willing to say hard things in hard situations because you're not concerned about how the person's response may detract from your sense of self-value. The quality of your speech will also improve when you use proper grammar and speak clearly and directly. You'll dress your age and keep yourself well-groomed because you have a proper perception of yourself, and you aren't trying to be something you're not.

While these qualities are important, the interior work you do is what matters most. Ultimately, this will have the greatest impact on the development of your exterior presence. People want a leader who comes across as genuine, authentic, and truly capable. Become someone worthy of trust, and make sure you follow through so that people are glad they trusted you.

Here's a few application questions as we wrap up:
1. What's the best element of your current executive presence?
2. What's one area where your executive presence could use some work?
3. How can you improve the quality of your interior life in a way that contributes positively to your executive presence?

For more about improving your executive presence, listen to Episode 129 of the StrongLead podcast.

Week 31: The Man in the Arena

In 1909, former President Theodore Roosevelt gave a stirring speech about responding to critics. During his speech, Roosevelt famously said,

> It's not the critic who counts, not the man who points out how the strong man stumbles or where the doer of deeds could have done them better. The credit belongs to the man who is actually in the arena, whose face is marred by dust and sweat and blood, who strives valiantly, who errs, who comes short again and again because there is no effort without error and shortcoming, but who does actually strive to do the deeds, who knows great enthusiasms, the great devotions, who spins himself in a worthy cause, who at the best knows in the end the triumph of high achievement, and who at the worst, if he fails, at least fails while daring greatly, so his place should never be with those cold and timid souls who neither know victory or defeat.

As a leader, you can probably think of several times in the past when you've faced outside criticism. There will always be cynics who want to point out shortcomings. We must take these comments with a grain of salt and remember that the critic isn't who counts.

To help you learn how to respond to criticism, here are four key principles to keep in mind. These ideas will help you lead yourself, your family, your business, and anywhere you find yourself fighting in the arena.

One: Do something

The world won't gradually get better (or even stay the same) without any effort. Unless you're willing to do something, your situation will never improve. Even if it's out of tune with how everyone around you is acting, your actions can have a tremendous impact on yourself and your surroundings.

Where do you feel called to act right now? What's at stake if you don't do anything?

Two: Expect cynics

Don't let yourself be surprised by critics. It'll be much easier to get thrown off your game. This can be especially hard for people-pleasers, but the fact of the matter is that everyone will have cynics. People can become cynical because they are lazy, they feel threatened, or they have different values. Some people truthfully just like to complain. Use wisdom to discern whether the feedback is coming from someone who wants to help you or if they just like to complain.

How can you prepare yourself to better respond to critics?

Three: Don't be a cynic

Criticizing is easy, but it's useless. It impacts your credibility and alienates you from the people around you. Fight the temptation to be a cynic, but don't go along with every evil or stupid idea. Remember, doing something good and wise is the best way to avoid doing something you shouldn't.

How can you adjust your attitude or expectations when you feel inclined to become cynical?

Four: Remember that cynics are not in the arena

You aren't fighting your cynics. They aren't even in the arena with you - they are on the sideline. Remember the cause you're fighting for and continue fighting despite what you hear from the outside.

What cause or effort is most important to you? What are you fighting for?

The best thing you can do is get in the arena and fight for a cause you believe in. You'll experience some defeats, but getting in the arena is the most impactful thing you can do. You must feel driven by the cause you serve and ignore the cynics as you give the fight everything you have.

For more about responding to critics, listen to Episode 128 of the StrongLead podcast.

Week 32: Leadership Is the Crucial Factor

Best-selling leadership author John Maxwell often says, "Everything rises and falls on leadership." While that sounds like an exaggeration, the statement holds true. Success and failure are determined by leadership.

Leadership is the crucial factor, and it's one you can ultimately control. These five steps will help you level up your leadership and make a difference in the teams and organizations you serve.

One: Embrace the fact that leadership matters
If we believe leadership matters, we'll give our leadership the attention it needs in order to grow. We'll also become more passionate about our leadership, and we'll be willing to continue to lead even when it gets hard.

If someone asked you to explain why leadership matters, what would you say?

Two: Acknowledge that you can grow as a leader
You're not stuck at your current level of leadership. Some people are naturally wired to be strong leaders, but many more people possess the potential to further grow and develop as a leader. If you're going to grow as a leader, you must acknowledge that you're not yet at your ceiling.

Imagine yourself as the best possible leader. What do you see? How can you take steps to grow in that direction?

Three: Conduct a leadership audit
Don't tune out when you hear the word "audit." This has nothing to do with taxes. Instead, this is an inventory of your current level of leadership. Think about where you should have influence and consider what results you desire. The final step is the most challenging, and it's identifying the gap between your ideal results and your current results.

How can you work to close the gap between your desired results and your present results?

Four: Invest in yourself as a leader
Putting time and money into your leadership is not selfish. Instead, it's being a good steward. At the end of the day, your leadership isn't about you. It's about the change or results that you create, which impacts everyone around you. When you invest in yourself, you're really investing in the outcomes you're working on.

How can you invest time, money, and energy into yourself as a leader?

Five: Make deliberate changes

It doesn't matter how much you know or how motivated you are. If you aren't putting things into practice, you won't move the needle. Recognize what you need to do to improve your leadership and execute the plan. It may be hard, but it's worth it.

What actions do you need to take to move forward in leadership?

Never forget that your leadership matters, no matter where you are or who you're leading. Make the most of your opportunities to lead, and do what you can to create a flourishing life all around you.

For more about strengthening your leadership, listen to Episode 126 of the StrongLead podcast.

Week 33: The Big Picture of Any Business

It's easy for business to become overcomplicated. We can get lost in the weeds or feel like we're drowning in countless details. Sometimes, it's helpful to step back and see the big picture to understand where business comes from.

No matter what industry you're in or how your business is structured, there are three intertwined functions involved in every business:

- **Sales.** This includes marketing, branding, and other tools you use to attract business.
- **Operations.** How do you provide products and services to your customers?
- **Support.** How are you supporting the people who are doing the selling and the operating? This category encompasses admin, HR, and other key roles.

Larger corporations may approach these areas in a more complicated fashion, but it's still helpful to think about your business through these lenses.

Thinking about your business from this perspective is helpful in four ways. Let's dig into each one below.

Perspective One: This lens assesses your business's health

What's the health of your business? Instead of diving into infinite details, you can take a high-level look to identify any potential bottlenecks. Are you getting tons of sales but struggling in operations? Are you doing well in sales and operations but not properly supporting your business? If your business is a system, this enables you to see where the system isn't running as smoothly as it could.

How healthy is your business right now? Where do you see bottlenecks?

Perspective Two: This lens provides orientation for employees

If you can communicate the way your business runs in simple terms, you'll have an easier time helping employees understand their unique purpose and function within your business. When employees feel like a cog in the machine, they won't see themselves as important, and they will be less likely to perform at their best.

How do you help employees see how they contribute to the larger purpose? How could you do a better job?

Perspective Three: This lens helps coordinate objectives between departments and teams

You'll be more effective when setting goals and planning initiatives if you can keep the entire team in mind. If you can involve different departments and team members from the beginning, that's even better. You'll streamline operations and design better products and services for your customers.

Perspective Four: This lens reduces your "turf wars"
"Turf wars" are internal battles where members of different departments fight against each other. Conflict is inevitable when human beings are working together. Without the big picture in mind, it's easy to feel like your department is the priority and everyone else is the enemy. As you move higher in your organization, you'll have to learn how to act and make decisions with everyone in mind.

The bottom line here is that you must train your team to see the big picture and operate accordingly. If you're not a top-level leader, try to play your role well with the big picture in mind. As you do this, you'll enhance your ability to serve in your role and stand out as someone with high potential.

For more about each business's core functions, listen to Episode 125 of the StrongLead podcast.

Week 34: Five Truths that Adults Accept

In ancient times, many cultures and people groups had various rites of passage that children would pass through in the process of becoming adults. These experiences would mark the transition between childhood and adulthood. These days, we don't have many rites of passage anymore, and many people find it more difficult to accept that they are no longer a child later in life.

What does it mean to be an adult? There are five truths inspired by Catholic priest Richard Rohr that further express what true adulthood looks like:

1. Life is hard
2. You are not that important
3. Life is not about you
4. You are not in control
5. You are going to die

While these five truths may first appear to be severely difficult realities, only children would deny their truth or believe the opposite. If you choose not to believe these truths, you have failed to embrace reality, and your refusal to embrace reality will create issues for yourself and those around you. This is normal for children but inappropriate for adults.

The timespan of transitioning into adulthood is taking longer these days than it has in previous years. The issue isn't only with millennials either -- people throughout different generations can struggle to accept these truths and live as adults. At the same time, your life will go much better if you can adjust to the reality represented by these truths, no matter how old you are. This doesn't necessarily mean that your life will be happier (see truth one), but it does mean that you'll find more goodness and richness in life.

So, what does this mean for leaders? How do you deal with somebody who is struggling to embrace these five truths? Here are five suggestions that may help:

- **Don't expect everyone to know all five truths fully.** Believing everyone should immediately understand all five truths reflects that you may not have fully accepted truth one ("life is hard").
- **Develop adults as a part of your job.** This may not feel like it should be your responsibility, and perhaps it's true. However, if you choose to accept this task, you'll play a role in contributing to a better workplace and society.
- **Never budge from these truths.** Don't change the job to fit people who are refusing to grow up. Do what you can to help people along so that they begin to grow up and embrace these truths.
- **Gently introduce these truths.** Say things like, "Here are some things adults know." Reaffirm them when

necessary. Don't use them as a weapon or share them in a passive-aggressive manner, but be honest about the negative implications of ignoring reality.

- **Model the way.** Show others what it looks like to live out these truths. Don't shy away from teaching when necessary, but remember that many things in life are caught and not taught.

When we notice that someone hasn't matured into an adult yet, we shouldn't hold it against them. However, if we never call them to a higher standard, we are accommodating them more than we should and holding them back from reaching their potential. Be patient with people while doing what you can to nurture them into adulthood.

Here are a few questions to consider as we wrap up:

1. Which of the five truths is most difficult for you to accept?
2. What's one step you can take to further embrace these truths on the path toward ongoing maturity?
3. Who is one person in your life struggling to become an adult? How can you help develop this person?

For more about being an adult in the workplace, listen to Episode 123 of the StrongLead podcast.

Week 35: Your Biggest Leadership Battles

Leadership can be a battle. Leaders fight against complacency, distractions, and many other things. However, your biggest battle as a leader is an internal battle. As leaders, we fight against the overwhelming temptation to believe that leadership is all about us.

What exactly does this mean? Well, oftentimes, we struggle with confusing the right way with our own preferred way. The right way might be what's best for your organization, but you may have another approach that you would like to take because of how it benefits or serves your interests.

Most people aren't purely selfish jerks. This type of person is pretty rare. What happens more often is we have an interest that doesn't reflect the highest good. It may have some value, but it doesn't support the highest purpose or goal of the business. We can't choose what's best for us as individuals over what's best for the business.

With this in mind, let's look at three common battlefronts where we must apply this principle:

One: The battle to "right-size" your role

There are two ends to this spectrum. On one end, you have the do-it-all person who wants to do everything. This person isn't actually leading. On the other end, you have the leader who delegates everything and does nothing himself or herself. A good leader is willing to delegate certain responsibilities that they would rather keep, and they are also willing to take on responsibilities that they would rather avoid. They don't deflect tasks because they feel like they are beneath them. As a leader, you can't function based solely on what you want. Instead, be willing to "right-size" your role in a way that serves the organization.

What's something you need to take responsibility for, even if you don't want to? And what's something you need to let go of while empowering someone else to take it on?

Two: The battle to give feedback well

Good feedback improves a person's performance or growth. Leaders who are more concerned about their own comfort will try to give feedback in a way that makes them feel better. These leaders may come across as overly harsh or aggressive when giving feedback, or they may sacrifice clarity by watering down the feedback in an attempt to avoid discomfort.

You should also avoid passive-aggressive feedback or inappropriately giving feedback to an individual in front of a group. Giving effective feedback is a battle, and it's one you must be willing to engage.

On a scale of 1 to 10, how do you rate your current ability to provide feedback? What would it take to raise your grade by 1-2 points?

Three: The battle not to take things personally

Many things happen in business or leadership that you could easily interpret as being personal. For example, if you're a manager and one of your employees shows up late for work, you could think the employee's tardiness is about you. You might see it as disrespectful or rebellious. Rarely (if ever) is this the case. Similarly, a sales manager whose team didn't hit their sales goal could feel that the team let the manager down in some personal way or that the team didn't work hard enough for the manager. In both cases, the manager is taking a circumstance personally.

When you make things about yourself, you diminish the quality of your leadership and stunt your growth. Instead of problem-solving that is focused on the real issues at hand, things get polluted with your own personal interpretations and concerns. When you free yourself from taking things personally, you are much better able to think clearly, be creative, and engage others fairly.

How often do you struggle with taking things personally? How can you shift your focus to make your leadership less about you?

As Russian author Alexander Solzhenitsyn once said, "The line between good and evil runs through the heart of every person." We're all fighting an internal battle between good and evil, and we must kill the seed of evil that comes from believing life is all about us. Recognize each battle in leadership as an opportunity to wage war against self-centeredness, and don't underestimate the value of authentic humility.

For more about facing battles as a leader, listen to Episode 122 of the StrongLead podcast.

Week 36: Four Keys to Being More Assertive

At its essence, leadership is influence. The goal is to influence other people to create outcomes that may not otherwise happen. While it would be great if people could read your mind or respond positively to all your requests, many people will not immediately want to follow you. If we're going to lead people well, we need to be assertive.

Being assertive is not the same thing as being aggressive. There's a key difference here. When you're aggressive, you're diminishing or disrespecting the other person. Leadership doesn't need to be overly personal. We also shouldn't be passive-aggressive, where we veil attacks in humor or ambiguity.

To be assertive is to be willing to stand up and articulate what's important. In many cases, what prevents us from being assertive is we conflate the other person's hurt feelings with our attitude or approach. We may disappoint people when we're assertive, but it doesn't mean that we're being rude or attacking people. In other words, it's not about the other person but about the outcome we're looking to achieve.

Here are four tips for any leader who wants to be more assertive.

One: Think in terms of being clear

A big part of being assertive is being clear about what you expect. If you're in a position of leadership, you should be clear about three specific things:

- **Goals.** Your goals are the reality you're trying to create.
- **Plans.** Your plans are your strategy for how you'll get to the goal.
- **Actions.** Your actions help you carry out your plan in pursuit of your goal.

You may remember when we talked about delegating within each of these areas in Week 21. Part of being clear is clarifying what role you want your team members to play in the development of goals, plans, and actions. Make sure they know whether they are being invited to come up with their own ideas or carry out your instructions.

How could you be more clear about goals, plans, and actions? What does it look like to be assertive in this area?

Two: Be assertive early and often

You should be assertive from the beginning about your expectations, and you should also be clear throughout the process whenever you're providing feedback. Whether or not things are going well, you should be clear and reinforce the standards you have in place. Remember that you may have to set expectations multiple times.

How can you improve your ability to be assertive throughout projects and initiatives?

Three: Don't make things overly emotional

When you make things personal, you become too consumed with yourself (as we discussed last week). If this comes out in your words or your non-verbal response, you can cause unnecessary tension between you and the other person. Rather than focusing on the issue, the focus will be on personal tension. As leaders, we must find the line between being assertive about things that matter to us without getting too worked up. This happens through the tone of our voice as well as how we interpret the actions of others. Remember, leadership is not about you.

How can you properly manage your emotions as you try to be more assertive?

Four: Start small

If you're not accustomed to being assertive, don't immediately overcorrect and become assertive about anything and everything. Find some areas where you can start small. Maybe you begin with a few people so you can practice, or you may initially limit the scope of things you're assertive about.

Being assertive starts with being clear. If you can find more opportunities to be clear as a leader, you'll eliminate confusion, keep your team on the same page, and move your organization to new heights.

For more about being more assertive, listen to Episode 121 of the StrongLead podcast.

Week 37: Three Commitments You Must Make

What's the first thing that comes to mind when you hear the word "commitment?" Perhaps you think about marriage, or maybe you envision sticking to a workout plan. The word commitment has a negative connotation for people who feel like commitment is overly difficult or something to be stuck with. Ultimately, commitment can be a very good thing, and your life will be richer and more impactful if you can develop a commitment to the right things.

As a leader, there are three commitments you should be willing to make. These commitments are important regardless of your rank in your organization, and you'll be a more effective leader by demonstrating these three commitments.

One: Be committed to a cause
You can be committed to more than one cause in your life, and commitments matter at work in the same way that they do in our personal lives. Typically, your business's cause is related to the purpose your company serves. This cause is something that is bigger than you, and if you're not committed to something beyond yourself, you're not truly leading. Without a greater cause

or purpose for leading, you'll be tempted to lead for selfish gain or pursuit and not for the benefit of the organization.

What cause are you committed to at work? How does a commitment to a cause manifest in the work your company does each day?

Two: Be committed to your own growth

When you serve a cause, it constantly requires you to grow and improve yourself. If you're truly committed to the cause, you'll be willing to do the hard work of growth and change so that you can better position yourself to serve within your role.

Many of the leaders we work with at StrongLead find that coaching helps them become less self-centered and more purpose-centered while also strengthening their confidence and sharpening their communication skills. Working in these areas isn't easy, which is why a commitment to growth matters.

What steps are you taking to grow and develop yourself? What impact does this have on your leadership?

Three: Be committed to bringing out the best from the people around you

To influence people to pursue outcomes that wouldn't happen otherwise, you have to recognize and utilize the strengths in your coworkers, team members, direct reports, leaders, and peers. If you work with someone, you should look to bring out the best in them.

If you oversee somebody, you're specifically responsible for bringing out the best performance from them while also helping them grow in a way that enhances their future performance.

Ultimately, if you're not committed to bringing out the best in others, you're not fully serving your cause or growing yourself.

What are some ways that you bring out the best in others around you? How could you further develop this skill?

Commitment is hard. If it wasn't, we wouldn't see many marriages ending in divorce, and people wouldn't give up on their workout plans after the first few weeks at the gym. It may not be easy work, but it's important, especially for anyone who wants to lead others and create positive change in their organization or their community. If you're willing to take on each of these commitments, you'll notice an incredible impact on yourself and the people around you.

For more about important leadership commitments, listen to Episode 120 of the StrongLead podcast.

Week 38: Making Business a Blessing

Is your business a blessing? Blessing can mean different things depending on the context. Ultimately, if your business is a blessing, you provide additional goodness for people by helping them flourish. At StrongLead, one of our mantras is to work people to life, not to death. We see workplaces all the time where people leave work worse than when they began. We believe that the workplace, when done right, can be much more of a blessing than a curse.

Let's look at three mental shifts that will help you define your business as a blessing.

One: Believe that work is good
When you believe that work is good, you're not attempting to trick yourself into believing a lie. Work truly is good. In the Bible, work existed before Adam and Eve disobeyed God and ate the fruit they were told to avoid. In addition, God did work in order to create the world. We must stop believing that work is a necessary evil. We don't just need the fruits of our labor, but we need the labor itself. If work isn't treated as good in your workplace, something may need to change.

How does it feel to think about work as good? How can you continue to make this mental shift and help your team members do the same?

Two: Believe that meaningless work is a curse

Work may be good, but not all work is created equal. In order to ensure that your business is a blessing, you should look to eliminate as much needless work as possible. The work you do each day should connect to your organization's cause or greater purpose.

This isn't only true for you, but it's true for the people who work under you. Whether it seems true or not, everyone cares about contributing to something greater than themselves. Do what you can to help people connect to the big picture, and since vision leaks, you should overcommunicate what your company is all about. This won't just lead to deeper engagement, but it will also honor the work that your team members do each day.

What meaningless tasks can you eliminate for yourself or for those who work with you?

Three: Foster love

Okay, so this one sounds kind of hippie or sappy. But fostering love isn't about wearing tie-dye T-shirts or bringing Valentine's Day cards for everyone in your office like you did back in elementary school. Instead, it's about creating an environment devoid of hate, envy, and gossip.

Too many leaders are shy about forcing their values onto the people they work with, and they feel like their workplace culture should remain neutral. The truth is that you're imposing your values on people, whether it's intentional or not.

If you don't share your values, you'll see weeds begin to grow in the form of negativity. Instead, look to create an environment fueled by the kind of love described by the late philosopher Dallas Willard: "Love is when I will good for someone else."

How can you bring a greater sense of love into the workplace?

If you pursue each of these mental shifts, you'll be the type of organization that works people to life and not to death. Your people will experience a greater sense of purpose and meaning when they come to work each day, and they will be better off because of the time they spend working alongside you.

For more about making business a blessing, listen to Episode 114 of the StrongLead podcast. This episode is the first in a six-part series on business as a blessing.

Week 39: Five Responsibilities You Can't Ignore

As a leader, you're probably better at some things than others. Regardless of what you might think, you're probably not naturally gifted at everything. Most of us tend to gravitate toward certain tasks because we enjoy doing them or because they are easy for us. Ultimately, your time is best spent when you can strike a balance between doing what you're good at and what your business needs from you.

As we think about what your business needs from you, let's look at five responsibilities you can't ignore as a leader. These are essential tasks that you can't abdicate. Even if you delegate them, you still must lead the charge and make sure they get done.

One: Building your team
You have to take responsibility for building your team. This means making sure your team has trust, alignment, and healthy conflict. You don't have to come up with all the team-building activities and facilitate the offsite on your own, but you can't sit on the sideline and watch all the team building happen. You should be the one to champion its importance and play a key role in the process.

What are you actively doing to build your team? What are you not currently doing that could help?

Two: Managing your direct reports

Some managers confuse managing with micro-managing and falsely assume that all managing is bad. It's a limiting belief that all managing is micro-managing, and it keeps too many leaders from properly supporting and helping their direct reports. It's your responsibility to help them address problems, keep them aligned, and set a direction for their work.

How are you managing your reports on an ongoing basis? How does this increase their current performance or future potential?

Three: Having difficult or uncomfortable conversations

There are some hard conversations that need to happen, and you're in charge of making them happen. Few things will lead to a loss of respect more quickly than asking others to initiate the conversations that you don't want to have.

What's your current attitude about difficult conversations? How does your ability to initiate hard conversations help (or hurt) your organization?

Four: Holding great meetings

Team meetings are one of the best times for work to get done. However, great meetings don't happen naturally - you have to play a role in making it happen. The best meetings are focused, intense, and relevant. Even if you aren't directly in charge of planning or leading the meeting, you can set the tone by communicating the importance of these three qualities and providing an example for others to follow.

How would you rate the effectiveness of your meetings on a scale of one to ten? How could you make them more focused, intense, and relevant?

Five: Communicating what matters

Your team needs you to articulate what matters. You can't have other people do this for you. Be prepared to repeat yourself to establish a high level of clarity. Why do you exist? Why do you do what you do? What's your vision? Where are you trying to go? What's our strategy? How will we get to where we want to go? These questions matter, and your employees need to hear the answers from you. Other leaders in your organization can echo this message, but they can't be the only people saying these things. It has to come from you first.

How often do you communicate your mission, vision, and strategy with your team? How can you continually reinforce these ideas?

Remember that delegating and shunning responsibilities are very different. Delegation is important, but you must never shun your essential responsibilities. You must take responsibility for the key tasks in your organization, even if you involve others in the process.

For more about essential leadership responsibilities, listen to Episode 113 of the StrongLead podcast.

Week 40: Four Essential Leadership Boundaries

A boundary is an expectation that you have for other people about how they treat you or act around you. These boundaries protect you, guard what's important to you, and help you be your best. Leaders need boundaries in order to be successful. In order to establish boundaries, leaders must clearly communicate and reinforce their boundaries.

Let's look at four boundaries all leaders must set:

One: Boundaries around focused work
Every leader has certain types of work that require a high level of uninterrupted concentration. The problem is that many leaders have an open-door policy that invites constant interruption. While an open-door policy can be a good thing in many situations, it leaves you vulnerable to interruption after interruption which prohibits you from doing a high level of work. You have to guard certain times and activities so you can focus, which could mean keeping your door closed at certain times, blocking off sections of your calendar, or working away from the office on occasion.

What times - or tasks - do you need to guard in order to bring a higher level of focus to your work?

Two: Boundaries around friendships at work

There's nothing wrong with having friendships at work, even with people you lead. However, you must remember that certain topics are out of bounds. You can't share everything with people you work with, and you should know when it's time to say that you can't say more about specific topics that may come up. We may establish real-world friendships by letting people in further than what's typical or expected, but this often isn't appropriate at work. To succeed at work, you'll need to bring some level of privacy into your workplace conversations.

How can you establish strong relationships at work without overstepping or oversharing?

Three: Outside obligations

When you're good at what you do, you'll get asked to do more work. You'll often have extra requests and opportunities coming your way. You may also feel tempted to chase rabbits and pursue shiny objects outside of your mission or vision. As a leader, you should be ready for these, and you should have clear boundaries about how you'll respond. This doesn't mean that you have to say "no" to everything, but you'll also have to determine how you'll say "no" to some things so you can say "yes" to the right things.

How do you decide whether to say "yes" or "no" to a new opportunity or obligation? How could you enhance these boundaries?

Four: Boundaries about how other people treat you

It's OK to set boundaries about things you don't like, whether that's regarding certain forms of language, topics of conversation, or personal privacy. You may have boundaries that other people don't have, and you may find that some people set up boundaries that you don't feel like you need. Whatever boundaries you choose to set, remember that other people can't read your mind, and you can't expect others to respect a boundary that you haven't clearly communicated or reinforced.

What's a personal boundary that's important to you even though others may not practice it themselves? What value does this boundary add?

Strong leaders are self-aware and comfortable in their own skin. Boundaries help these leaders be who they are. If you're going to be a high-level leader who has a strong impact, you can't simply go with the flow. You must guard the things that are important to you, and boundaries will help you do this.

For more about setting boundaries in leadership, listen to Episode 110 of the StrongLead podcast.

Week 41: Delegating Like a Champ

Many leaders struggle to delegate properly, but an inability to delegate effectively will hold you back in leadership. A good leader seeks to multiply their ability and there is no better way to do that than to become a highly effective delegator. In Week 21, we talked about three layers of delegation. For this week's entry, let's take a look at seven steps you can take to improve your delegation.

One: Reframe a lack of delegation as something a loser would do

Some leaders view doing everything as a badge of honor, but this is a dangerous and shortsighted perspective. Other leaders think that delegating is a sign of laziness. Truth is, delegation isn't a sign of weakness, it's a strategy for being more efficient and effective. Leaders are expected to delegate because delegation is how things get done.

What limiting beliefs or false narratives might hold you back from delegating more often?

Two: Understand delegation as a skill

Nobody comes out of the womb able to delegate. Like any skill, it's one that you have to learn over time. It's not easy, but it's worth the effort to learn and develop competence.

How can you improve your ability to delegate? What would it take to get better?

Three: Delegate for others' growth

Some leaders avoid delegation because it seems like it would take too long. It's true that some things would be quicker to do on your own, but delegating often builds capacity and ability for the person to whom you're delegating. In other words, you're not delegating to get tasks done, but you're delegating for the other person's long-term capacity and benefit.

Whose ongoing growth and development could benefit if you delegated more to them?

Four: Stop being a control freak

If you want to delegate like a champ, you must ask yourself why you're holding onto certain tasks. Fear shouldn't hold you back from delegating. Let go of the need to control everything or the idea that you're the only person who can do something. Remember that the higher up you go in leadership, the less you'll be responsible for tasks and the more accountable you'll be for producing results.

What tasks are most difficult for you to delegate? What makes this challenging?

Five: Be ready for resistance

You might delegate something to someone who initially resists
or refuses. This could be a sign that you have a people problem
in your organization. Just like leaders must be able to delegate,
team members should be competent at accepting delegation.
You must work to set the tone and educate your employees
about how to respond when something is delegated to them.
This will be more effective if you communicate the importance
of accepting delegation early and often.

How will you equip your team members to accept delegation?

Six: Focus more on what to do than how to do it.

"What" is more general than "how." For example, what a car
dealership manager wants is to sell cars in a way that makes
money for the business while keeping customers happy and the
dealership's reputation strong. How exactly a particular
salesperson does this with a given customer is largely up to the
salesperson because the dealership manager has delegated selling
cars to the salespeople.

When it comes to delegating, you want to focus more on what to
do than how exactly to do it because you need decision-makers
at the "how" level. If a person isn't capable of deciding how to
do something, they are not ready for the assignment to be
delegated to them. When a person is capable of deciding how to
do the assignment, they are empowered and ready for delegation.
By focusing more on what needs to be done than on how exactly
to do it, you're empowering people to be decision-makers and
shortening the time it takes to delegate tasks.

*When you think about tasks with a clear "what" and a "how" that could
be delegated, what comes to mind?*

Seven: Get organized

It's nearly impossible to delegate well if you're running in 100 different directions and reacting to whatever is urgent. If you don't have your priorities clear, you won't delegate well. If you can take the necessary steps to get organized, you'll be able to delegate more often and more effectively.

What's one step you could take to get more organized?

As a leader, you serve an important cause bigger than yourself. Your organization exists for a purpose, and this cause depends on your ability to delegate. If you don't choose to delegate, you'll hold back the cause and create unnecessary friction. Improving your ability to delegate will help you better fulfill your purpose.

For more about effective delegation, listen to Episode 109 of the StrongLead podcast.

Week 42: Going Negative

Do you know somebody who is always negative? Maybe they are constantly complaining, shooting down ideas, or acting as a taskmaster who feels like nothing is ever good enough. These behaviors can quickly become toxic and push others away. However, there are certain times when it's good to be negative as a leader.

Negativity creates conflict, and conflict is important because it can be corrective. People may avoid negativity because they don't enjoy this type of dissonance, but an over-avoidance of negativity can cause you to let certain behaviors and attitudes continue when they shouldn't. If you're going to get your team moving in the right direction, you'll need to learn when – and how – to be negative.

Here are three situations when it's appropriate, as a leader, for you to be negative:

- **When there is underperformance.** If there's an employee, team, or division that is underperforming or not hitting a goal, negativity will help you point out the gap and call the team (or the team member) to a higher standard. This conversation doesn't always have to stay in a negative place, but it can feel this way when you initially point out the underperformance.

- **When somebody is out of bounds.** If there is an ethical concern or if an employee steps outside of the company's core values, you can't let it go unaddressed. If you don't go negative here, people will continue to push boundaries or assume you don't really value what you say you do.
- **When there's been a loss or major setback.** Perhaps you lost a major client or donor, or maybe you didn't get a project you bid on. This negativity is less about correction and more about reflecting the appropriate level of disappointment or frustration to reinforce that the loss wasn't what you wanted.

Which situation comes up most often in your team or organization? How can you appropriately respond with the right amount of negativity?

Now that you know when you should be negative, you may wonder what effective negativity looks like. Here are four important reminders:

- **Don't confuse negative energy with low energy.** Your voice could be high or low. You could be talking more or less. Negativity goes beyond your tone or posture.
- **Keep it in proper proportion.** Research from Barb Fredrickson of UNC-Chapel Hill shows that team performance is highest when the ratio of positive to negative interactions is between 3:1 and 10:1. You can be too positive, but you can much more easily become too

negative if you overcorrect. If you're at a 1:1 right now, you need to bring in more positivity. If you're overly positive, watch for situations where negativity might be appropriate.

- **Don't get emotionally negative.** Emotions can be negative, but when you're going negative with someone else based on your emotions, the other person is likely to focus more on your emotions than on the issue at hand. Intense anger can diminish your message. You can be frustrated, but keep the conversation focused on performance or the issue at hand.

- **Some behaviors are always toxic and should be avoided.** Negativity can be beneficial, but being passive-aggressive is never appropriate or helpful. The same is true for sarcasm for corrective purposes. It may be acceptable when talking about politics but not when discussing employee performance. Avoid flamethrowing or overwhelming people with negative energy in an attempt to burn them or cut them down to size.

What are 1-2 steps you can take to improve your ability to be negative based on the four reminders you just read above?

If you're not going negative often enough, you're probably not doing your job as effectively as you could. Most leaders want to be nice and have good emotional intelligence, but sometimes you must bring in the right amount of negativity in order to help people be their best.

For more about when it's OK to be negative, listen to Episode 108 of the StrongLead podcast.

Week 43: Three Disciplines You Don't Want to Overdo

Discipline is important, but some disciplines can be overdone or overemphasized. Your success as a leader depends on your ability to practice these disciplines without taking them too far. Let's explore three disciplines that should be on your radar but also be kept in check.

One: Self-Discovery
Self-discovery is about getting in tune with your identity and being aware of what values drive you. All leaders should engage in some level of self-discovery. If you haven't done any self-discovery, you'll easily fold when things get hard.

At the same time, if you take self-discovery too far, you can become overly arrogant. You might begin to expect others to drop their identity and embody yours. You may also view yourself as the primary point of reference in the world and the guidepost for what's right and what's wrong. This can quickly harm your leadership and push people away. If you can figure out how to practice the proper amount of self-discovery, you won't become too self-absorbed and expect others to see the world exactly as you do.

How engaged are you in ongoing self-discovery? How would you know if you were doing too much internal introspection?

Two: Diversity

Diversity means understanding what's important to groups of people and trying to meet everyone's needs. It's important to appreciate all people and the unique perspectives they bring, but it's still possible to overappreciate different groups if we aren't careful. When we do this, we bring our organization into chaos, confusion, and fragmentation. The presence of diverse values can diminish the core values that bring your team together. You might run the risk of overpromising in an attempt to meet all the different needs, which can produce even more confusion.

How can you value and affirm diversity without creating chaos and confusion?

Three: Support

As a leader, your people need direction and support from you. Direction is telling them what to do while supporting is the relational piece of leading others. It's important for you to bring encouragement, hope, and optimism to your team. You can even offer a listening ear and a helping hand on occasion. The problem is that if you bring too much support, you can foster a culture of dependency where people stop getting stronger and instead rely on you to help them get everything done. If things don't improve, you'll end up creating a situation where you're doing someone else's job in addition to your own.

How can you bring the proper amount of support to your employees while still empowering them to stretch and grow?

Exercising these three disciplines is important for anyone who wants to lead others. However, you also need to bring wisdom and discernment to the table with you. Watch out for signs that you might be overdoing it in one of these three areas, and be willing to course correct and dial it back when necessary.

For more about disciplines you shouldn't overdo, listen to Episode 107 of the StrongLead podcast.

Week 44: Four Qualities People Expect from Leaders

We often talk about what leaders expect from followers, but when was the last time you stopped to think about what followers expect from their leader? You can't be a leader without followers because leadership is relational at its essence. People aren't required to follow a leader, but they choose to follow a leader because the leader has earned their respect and trust.

Let's dig into four qualities followers expect from leaders. If you lack any one of these four categories, you shouldn't be surprised when people hesitate to follow you.

One: Honesty
Nobody follows without trust, and nobody should trust without honesty. In order to lead well, you must be honest. Honesty goes beyond overtly lying and extends into telling the full truth. Leaders can't shade or hide parts of the truth, even if it's for perceived noble reasons. This is manipulation, and people can see through it regardless of your reasons. If you want people to trust and follow you, you have to be clear and direct, even when it's not easy. You should also keep the promises you make and follow up on the things you say you'll do.

*How do you practice honesty in your leadership? How could you grow
in this area?*

Two: Forward-looking

As a leader, you're taking people somewhere, and they are
looking to you to tell them where you're going. If people don't
have a compelling future or a reason for moving forward, they
won't go anywhere. They need direction, and it's your job as a
leader to bring people toward an appealing future that's worth
the effort needed to get there.

*As a leader, where are you taking people? How often do you communicate
this vision with your team?*

Three: Inspiring

The leader's enthusiasm must be contagious. Even if you don't
have natural charisma, you should understand the emotional side
of leading. Typically, humans are not logically driven entities like
computers. They are driven by emotions, and strong leaders help
people feel deeply and experience these emotions in a way that
helps them commit to action.

*How do you inspire your team on an ongoing basis? What's the emotional
appeal you share that encourages those around you to act?*

Four: Competent

To lead well, you have to be seen as somebody who is capable
and effective. You don't have to be perfect, but others do need
to view you as someone who sees things accurately and can
effectively make decisions that require wisdom. You should also
have some level of business or technical competency that relates

to what your role requires. If people don't believe you're competent, they won't want to follow you.

How would you rate your current level of competency? Does this competency invite people to follow you, or does it push people away?

As you think about these competencies, consider which one you most need to develop. You don't have to be perfect in every area, but you should be working to grow in each domain so that you'll become a leader who people want to follow. Commit to growth in these four areas, and you'll continue to invite people to follow you not from a sense of obligation but because you've gained their trust.

For more about the qualities people expect from leaders, listen to Episode 106 of the StrongLead podcast.

Week 45: Care Enough to Confront

When was the last time you confronted someone? Try to think about a professional situation and not a scenario that involves family. It could have been a vendor, a teammate, a boss, or someone who reports to you. You confronted them by bringing a situation to their attention and making them face it even if it's uncomfortable.

Confrontation is important because things can get in the way of the growth of our companies and our own leadership capacity. If we're going to lead well, we must learn how to confront appropriately. Proper confrontation is better than ignoring issues, accepting mediocrity, or confronting in a way that leads to a bigger mess. Unhelpful confrontation is when we challenge the person in a way that creates more drama or comes across as overly personal.

If we're going to be good at confrontation, there are three things we must care about. Let's look at each one below.

One: Care about the cause

Ultimately, leadership is about serving a cause. This could be your company's overarching purpose or a long-range goal you have for your organization. If you care enough about the cause, you must be willing to wade into the discomfort, knowing it's uncomfortable for both you and the person you are confronting. If you care more about feelings than the cause, you won't be willing to confront them. You must be willing to sacrifice comfort in order to serve the cause that matters to you. You must also be willing to talk regularly about your values so that everyone is clear about the main goal.

How much do you care about the cause? Is your level of care supporting (or diminishing) your ability to confront important matters?

Two: Care about the other person

Unless you're in a family, the cause always outweighs the other person. Still, even in a business or other professional setting, you must care about the other person if you're going to confront well. The other person matters, and how they experience the confrontation will determine the results. The confrontation will only be effective if the other person hears and receives it well and responds appropriately.

Don't get discouraged if the confrontation doesn't initially feel positive. There's probably going to be a sense of awkwardness or negativity at first. However, this can give way to more pleasant feelings when collaboration ensues, and you start working on a solution with the other person. We can't act as if confrontation is good news, nor can we diminish people's feelings, and we should acknowledge that what we have to say may be hard to hear.

How can you bring more care into confrontations? How would this produce more beneficial outcomes for everyone involved?

Three: Care about the relationship

If you don't confront them, you'll eventually reach a place of contempt where the relationship starts to sour. You don't want to reach a point where you can't stand being around the other person. Because you care about the person and the relationship, you're willing to bring up something difficult and help the person face the issue at hand. Remember, healthy relationships have some degree of confrontation.

How could effective confrontation enhance the quality of your relationships at work?

As we wrap up, recognize that confronting is not the same thing as controlling. You can't control other people, and the other person will always get to choose whether they want to make the adjustments or not. There may be times when you confront well, and the other person still doesn't react in a positive way. Still, there are times when confrontation is necessary for the continued health of your organization.

Keep these things in mind the next time you confront someone and when you are confronted by someone else.

For more about caring enough to confront, listen to Episode 105 of the StrongLead podcast.

Week 46: Five Ways to Gain Wisdom

What is wisdom? It's a word we use often, but we don't always fully grasp what it means. Essentially, wisdom is good judgment. It isn't a substitute for knowing the rules, it isn't simple intuition, and it's not a substitute for collecting data or gathering information.

However, wisdom enables us to make good contextual decisions. Sometimes, leaders want to fall back on rules and policies. The issue is that everyday life often isn't this cut and dry. If we possess wisdom, we'll know how to apply rules and policies in complex situations that don't have obvious answers.

The other challenge with wisdom is it requires us to think. We'll never be able to create enough policies to eliminate the need for wisdom. Maybe you have policies and procedures for how to handle situations with troubled employees, but wisdom will tell you how to handle the situation with that individual employee by considering all relevant factors.

There are many situations in our everyday lives that require the use of wisdom, which makes the development of wisdom crucial

for everyone, but especially leaders. Let's think about a few ways
that you can pursue greater wisdom.

One: Experience

There's no substitute for lived experience. Wisdom often comes
with age, but it often comes from successes and failures. These
experiences provide wisdom that you can apply to future
situations and share with others.

What experiences in life have produced the most wisdom for you?

Two: A willingness to learn from experience

Time alone doesn't make you wise, but a willingness to learn
from past experiences does. Failing and stumbling are great
teachers. A young child learning how to walk needs to fall
hundreds (perhaps thousands) of times before they can
consistently walk. These experiences teach them how to stand
upright. Learning from your mistakes requires humility and a
willingness to examine past failures to see what you could have
done better.

*How easy is it for you to learn from past experiences? If this is hard for you,
what would it take to improve?*

Three: Learn from other people's experience

You can learn from others' mistakes even if you don't make the
same mistake yourself. See what you can gather from talking
with people, listening to others' stories, and hearing what
perspective they have to share.

Who do you know that's wise? How could you learn from this person?

Four: Reflect and review

Sometimes, it's good to take a time out and review your past progress. Ask questions like "What went well," "What could I have done differently," and "What did I learn?" If you never take time to step back and review, you'll never soak in the lessons that are all around you. Instead, take time to reflect on what's happened so you can move forward with greater wisdom.

When would be a good time for you to step back, review, and see what wisdom you can gain?

Five: Seek wisdom

The Biblical book of Proverbs says that the beginning of wisdom is to get wisdom. If we aren't pursuing wisdom, it won't come to us accidentally. When we value wisdom, we're willing to do whatever is necessary to find it.

How can you turn your attention to wisdom so that it's more apparent when you see it?

If you're not already in a leadership position, you'll attract attention from others when you exercise wisdom. Be wise, and you'll find doors beginning to open for you. If you're already leading others, don't forget that people want to follow the wise. You'll be more impactful and influential as a leader if others can sense that you're acting wisely.

For more about when you must show courage, listen to Episode 101 of the StrongLead podcast.

Week 47: Workplace Celebration

There are specific times and reasons when workplace celebration is important. It's easy for leaders to avoid celebration or write it off as lost productivity, but celebration can have tremendous value for you and the people you work with when it's done well. Let's discuss what, why, who, and how to celebrate at work.

What should we celebrate?
You can celebrate several things at work. Victories are a great cause for celebration. It will look different for each company, but whether it's a big sale, a key hire, or a new building, it's worth taking the time to celebrate.

Milestones are also opportunities to celebrate. So are the completion of hard seasons and notable expressions of your core values. When you reach these critical junctures, don't just put your head down and keep moving forward. First, pause and take a moment to celebrate what took place.

What victories and milestones could your company celebrate?

Why celebrate?

We celebrate because human beings have a need for story. They need to find a sense of accomplishment in the work they do. People must feel like they are going somewhere and that what they are doing matters. Celebrating brings the "why" out in work and fosters a greater sense of teamwork between you and the people you work with.

How can celebration bring your team together and reinforce your purpose or cause?

Who should we celebrate?

You could have a company-wide celebrations, but such a celebration will likely miss the mark unless you're in a smaller company. Oftentimes, the celebrations with the greatest impact focus on specific individuals and teams. Leaders sometimes avoid these types of celebrations because they don't want to make others feel bad, but if you never highlight strong contributions, you'll always have mediocre people. Remember, what gets rewarded gets repeated, and what you acknowledge communicates what you care about most.

What individual or team should you celebrate, both to honor the individual(s) and to reinforce your company values?

How should we celebrate?

You don't always have to throw a big party, especially if the person you're celebrating is more introverted. Cater to individual preferences as much as possible when celebrating, with one exception: consider going slightly more public than what they would prefer. This isn't solely about the individual's feelings but about showing the celebration to the rest of the team because it reinforces what's important in your company. It's also about allowing others to enjoy the celebration alongside the individual and not about making them feel inferior or inadequate because they aren't the ones being celebrated.

Think about the next time you have a reason to celebrate in your company. How will you mark the occasion?

Make an effort to celebrate something over the next thirty days. It may not seem obvious right now what you should celebrate, but when you sit down to think about it, you will identify something worth acknowledging. The more you practice celebrating, the better job you will do and the more reasons you'll have to celebrate within your company.

For more about celebrating accomplishments at work, listen to Episode 100 of the StrongLead podcast.

Week 48: Leading Where You Are

A person can lead – at least to some degree – regardless of the position they hold in the organization. While it's easy to acknowledge this truth when it comes to others, you need to embrace it for yourself, as well.

Perhaps you're not at the top of the organizational chart and you don't sit in a corner office. No matter where you are, you can lead others, and if you want to be the best version of yourself, you have to learn how to lead where you are. You can't wait to be promoted before you start leading.

There are seven ways you can lead, regardless of your position. These may seem like basic tips, but leaders are the ones who are willing to do the most elementary tasks, even when it seems like they should be obvious. These are the tasks that everyone should be doing, but few people are willing to do.

One: Never be late
You've probably heard it said that to be early is to be on time, and to be on time is to be late. If you want to lead where you are, take your current role and team seriously. One of the best

ways to demonstrate this is to be early, meet deadlines, and respect others' time whenever possible. Don't be the one people are waiting on.

Two: Take care of little things

Every company has little things that need to be done. This includes detail-oriented work like paperwork, follow-through, and extra phone calls. These tasks aren't necessarily fun, but they make a major difference. Too few people are willing to do these things, and you'll stand out if you're willing to step up to the plate and make sure they get done.

Three: Take care of dirty work

There's some overlap between little things and dirty work, and they both matter. Somebody has to clean the coffee pot and replace the toilet paper. You'll find these tasks in every work environment, and you'll make an impression if you're the one who's willing to take care of these things as you go.

Four: Ask for feedback

Be willing to receive feedback and respond by incorporating what you hear into your work. Many employees just want to get by and do the bare minimum. When you ask for feedback, you're communicating a willingness to grow and a desire to help the organization.

Five: Shut down gossip

Shutting down gossip goes well beyond avoiding participation in gossip. You must be the one who's willing to stand up and put a stop to gossip when it's going on. People enjoy drama, but there's no place for this type of talk in a serious business. This is a great space to give feedback appropriately and respectfully to others, even if you're not in a formal leadership role.

Six: Admit your mistakes

Everyone makes mistakes. If you're going to model the way for others to follow, you should be willing to admit your mistakes. Some people will cringe when you do this because they are more concerned with looking good than helping the company. Effective leaders avoid this game because they are looking for the performance needed to get the job done. Errors will happen, and the best thing you can do to move forward is to admit what happened and move on.

Seven: Be willing to stand out for the right things

We all face the temptation to fit in, but this won't help you on your journey to becoming the best leader possible. A strong leader is willing to go against the grain and stand out for doing the right thing. One way to do this is by embodying and standing up for your company values. This can make people uncomfortable depending on the context, but leaders are willing to make sacrifices in pursuit of the company's values and its key cause.

Doing these seven things isn't about getting ahead. It's more about living in your circle of influence and taking care of what is under your care. When you do this well, your circle of influence grows. As your circle of influence expands, along with new responsibilities, you'll also find greater happiness and satisfaction.

A few questions as we wrap up:
1. Which principle is easiest for you to practice? Which is most difficult?
2. Which principle could have the greatest impact on you and your team?
3. How can you grow in your ability to lead where you are?

For more about leading where you are, listen to Episode 99 of the StrongLead podcast.

Week 49: Three Fears You Must Overcome

Fear is natural and normal. Fear keeps us from driving at 150 miles per hour, from jumping off cliffs, and from seeing if that wild mushroom is tasty. At the same time, fear also holds many people back from being strong leaders. If you're going to lead at your best, you must learn how to recognize fear and overcome it. More specifically, all leaders must overcome three fears.

One: Making tough decisions

You might remember when we talked about FOMAD ("Fear of Making a Decision") in Week 14. The reality is that life is full of decisions, and leaders are called to make decisions daily. As you rise in leadership, many smaller decisions will be delegated to others, but you'll still be in charge of making the toughest decisions.

Some leaders get held back from making tough decisions by over-relying on data. They never make a decision because they feel like they haven't done enough research or consulted with enough experts. Ultimately, if you have all the data, there's no real decision to make. You only make decisions when you don't have a sufficient number of facts. If you fear making decisions because you don't want to make a wrong decision, you'll always stay stuck.

When you lack data but still have to make a decision, you can fall back on principles and experience. If you can't back up a decision on principles or experience, you may just need to go with your gut. Imagine the best version of yourself and what decision you would make in that space. This draws on your internal strength and clarifies what the right direction could be.

How much fear do you feel when it comes time to make a decision? How would you like to respond to that fear?

Two: Making an enemy
We always prefer to make friends, but we must overcome the fear of making enemies every once in a while. More often than not, this fear is unfounded. We may disappoint or disagree with people, but the eventual outcome isn't as dangerous or impactful as we thought. At the same time, if we're always afraid of making enemies or concerned with pleasing people, we may not stand up for what's right or hold people accountable.
When we act in a way that reflects our values, even when others may not agree, we often garner more respect along the way. Of course, we must be sure that our way is the right way. If you do the hard work of discernment and strongly feel that you're making the right decision, you'll be willing to lead through it, even if you make an enemy or two in the process.

How does the fear of making enemies impact your work and your decisions?

Three: Making a personal change

Take a minute to think about who you are. What needs to change? We fear admitting these things to ourselves and others because we don't want to feel or look weak. However, strong leaders reshape reality, and that includes the reality of who you are. As a leader, you must be willing to change people for the better, starting with yourself.

What about you needs to change? How will you go about making that change?

Everyone is afraid at times, but strong leaders can summon the courage to face their fear and press through it. They don't ignore it and hope it will go away. They are willing to embrace fear and move forward in courage. How can you become this type of leader?

For more about overcoming fears, listen to Episode 96 of the StrongLead podcast.

Week 50: Holding Others Accountable

Holding people accountable is a challenge for many leaders, but it's one of the most important tasks in leadership. Accountability is a form of influence, and leaders utilize every form of influence available – even those forms they find uncomfortable or awkward.

Even when we don't enjoy it, accountability is necessary for supervising, managing, and leading. Let's discuss a few dos and don'ts when it comes to holding someone accountable who is underperforming, whether that underperformance has to do with outcomes or process.

One: Get your mind right
You must think properly about accountability before you can actually hold people accountable. This starts with recognizing that resisting accountability is a bigger failure than the behavior you're addressing with the other person. Instead, you should create a culture of accountability by normalizing it in your brain and your business.

You can do this without damaging relationships or hurting other people. Never forget that the underperformance is the source of the hurt, not you. In fact, no part of accountability is about you. It's not personal – it's about performance.

What is your current perspective on accountability? How is it helping -- or hurting -- your leadership?

Two: Get your timing right

Timely accountability doesn't happen at annual performance reviews. You should be evaluating performance, offering feedback, and checking in throughout the year. If something doesn't meet expectations, you need to call it out and talk about it as you go. Only offering feedback once a year is not effective, mainly because if the underperformance truly mattered, you wouldn't let it go unaddressed for long periods. If you don't leverage the moment, you won't have the best possible impact.

How can you do a better job of providing timely, constructive feedback?

Three: Get your words right

Some leaders want to skip ahead and think about what to say when holding others accountable, but this can't happen unless you first get your mind and timing right. When it comes time to have the conversation, there are several best practices to emulate:

- **Keep your emotions in check.** If you're too emotional, people won't hear your message. Don't make feedback overly personal and do your best to avoid sarcasm and passive aggression.

- **Don't substitute talking *to* people with talking *about* people.** Talking to someone else to prepare for a hard conversation is fine. Engaging in gossip in an attempt to avoid holding people accountable is not.

- **Speak to the person individually.** If one person needs to hear the feedback, don't speak to a group of ten people. The individual may assume you're not talking to them, and others can tell you're trying to avoid a difficult one-on-one.

- **Don't ask for – or make – excuses.** A better approach is to help the person identify obstacles and coach them through how to address the obstacles.

- **Be clear about your desired result.** You're not necessarily looking for agreement. You're looking for understanding and clarity about the expectation.

Think about a time when you gave constructive feedback that was received well. What can you learn from that situation?

Accountability doesn't matter if what you're doing doesn't matter. If you don't care about the cause for which your organization exists, you don't have to worry about holding anyone accountable. On the other hand, if you have a cause you care deeply about, it's worth getting accountability right, and you'll get better at it as you get more practice.

For more about holding others accountable, listen to Episode 94 of the StrongLead podcast.

Week 51: How Leaders Lose Respect

You shouldn't pursue a leadership role because you want or need respect. Leadership doesn't lead to respect, but respect does lead to stronger leadership. Since leadership involves influencing people to pursue an outcome or in service to a cause, we must have some degree of respect for the people we lead. Otherwise, we won't have any followers.

The problem is too many leaders do things that lose respect. Below, you'll read about three ways that leaders often lose respect. We'll also talk about how you can do the opposite of each of these things in your own leadership.

One: Failing to set clear expectations
When you boil leadership down to its bare bones, it's setting a goal and motivating others to take action in pursuit of that goal. You may say something like, "This is where we're going, and here's what I need from you," and both of these aspects require strong clarity. Leaders lose respect when they don't set clear expectations, and it can create strong tension between you and the people you lead. You might feel like you have an

underperforming employee when the reality is the employee
doesn't know what they are supposed to do because you haven't
told them yet.

*How effectively do you set expectations for those you lead? How could you be
even more clear about what you expect?*

Two: Failing to hold people accountable

Last week, we talked at length about how we can do a better job
of setting people accountable. Leaders avoid holding people
accountable for many reasons. Some leaders are busy with other
tasks or would simply rather work in other areas. It's important
to remember that holding people accountable is often urgent
and important, which means that it deserves our attention in a
timely manner.

Others don't want to be uncomfortable or aren't sure how the
other person will respond. Even though accountability isn't easy,
we'll quickly lose respect if we avoid doing hard things. Keep in
mind that the responsibility to hold people accountable includes
holding yourself, as the leader, accountable as well.

*Think about a time when you avoided holding someone accountable. What
was motivating you? How could you respond differently in the future?*

Three: Failing to reward good performance

In the same way that you must hold people accountable, you
should reward strong performance. If you need help learning
how to celebrate at work, go back and reread Week 45's entry on
celebration. Maybe you avoid celebration because you don't
want people to get too complacent or comfortable. What will
actually happen is you'll lose the respect of your team (and you

may risk losing some of your top performers as well). On the other hand, when you recognize the type of performance you desire, you'll get more of it.

How can you do a better job of rewarding good performance at work? What sort of impact would this have?

At the end of the day, leadership isn't about you. Having respect also isn't about you, but it will help you better serve your cause. Leading well requires some level of respect, and it's on you to earn and maintain that respect.

For more about maintaining respect, listen to Episode 93 of the StrongLead podcast.

Week 52: Four Reasons People Come to Work

We've come a long way since we began nearly one year ago. We've talked about vision, delegation, accountability, and so many other crucial leadership topics. As we wrap up with one final entry, it's important to look at work through the eyes of the people that we lead so we can understand how to best lead them. Let's close out this hands-on leadership guide by reminding ourselves of the four main reasons why people come to work.

One: A paycheck

We can idealize work and make it out to be something magical, but money is the most basic need people have for seeking out jobs. You shouldn't shy away from this truth as a manager. A job is an exchange of value: people put forth effort in exchange for a paycheck. It's not the only reason why people work, but it's one of the most fundamental – especially in lower-wage jobs.

Think about your first job as a teenager or young adult. What motivated you to work? Was it the paycheck or something else?

Two: Relationships

A paycheck may be essential, but it's not enough. It's why employees come, but it's not why they stick around year after year. People find greater value in work from the relationships they create. Relationships can't replace a paycheck, but it's the next thing people desire after the paycheck. If you have an environment with toxic relationships or condescending management, people won't want to work in your company. On the other hand, the stronger the relationships are, the stronger the workplace environment will be.

How would you rate the quality of the relationships in your workplace? What could you do to make them better?

Three: A chance to exercise strengths

We're beginning to move from needs to desires. Everyone wants to be good at what they do. After people know they have a paycheck and feel like they have strong relationships, they want to feel proficient or skilled at their job. Research shows that when someone feels a level of mastery at a skill, their sense of self-worth goes up.

Think about the people who work for you or with you. How often are they working in their strengths? What kind of worth or value do they receive from doing what they do?

Four: A sense of meaning

People come to work because they want to feel like they are a part of something bigger than themselves. They want to feel like the work they are doing creates meaning for them and for others. Not everyone experiences this, but every job has the potential to satisfy this desire for people. It's more challenging in some positions than others, but leaders can strive to make every job more meaningful. Help your team members see the connection between what they do day in and day out and how it creates additional good in the world. Talk about the vision of the company and let them feel like they are part of a story that is bigger and more meaningful than simply coming to work every day.

How can you bring an additional sense of fulfillment or satisfaction to the people working on your team?

As a leader, do what you can to make work worthwhile for people by meeting these needs to the best of your abilities. Doing so will benefit your business in more ways than one. You'll be more productive and profitable, but you'll also do a better job of working people to life instead of death.

For more about why people come to work, listen to Episode 85 of the StrongLead podcast.

Conclusion and Next Steps

Leadership is a never-ending journey. We've come a long way in 52 weeks, but this is just the beginning. The call to lead is a call to constant reflection, evaluation, and self-improvement. This isn't because you feel inadequate or because you're trying to prove something to yourself or others. Instead, it's because the cause or purpose you're serving demands your absolute best.

With this in mind, how can you continue growing as a leader now that you've finished reading this book? First of all, you can subscribe to the StrongLead podcast. Each week, we record a new episode designed to help you become a stronger leader. The content is very similar to what you've engaged with here, and we think you'll find it insightful and valuable on your journey to becoming a better leader.

We'd also love to walk alongside you and help develop your leaders. In working with hundreds of businesses, we've learned that each organization has people problems they must solve. These issues include (but are not limited to) motivation, turnover, employee engagement, unhealthy conflict, poor

decision-making, and a low sense of ownership. If you ignore
these problems, they won't go away. In fact, they will probably
get worse.

Thankfully, there's a way to get rid of your people problems
without getting rid of your people, and we would love to help.
We specialize in growing your people and helping you build a
strong company culture that can achieve greater success and
produce a more substantial impact. Here's how we would
proceed:

- **Facing the challenge.** We'll help you assess your needs
  and develop a plan. Once the plan is finished, we'll get to
  work.
- **Grow your people.** Based on what your plan dictates,
  we'll provide coaching and training where your team
  needs it the most.
- **Shrink your problems.** As your people grow, your
  problems will shrink, and your business will become
  more profitable and prosperous.

If this interests you, head over to our website at stronglead.org
to schedule your free 90-minute consultation. This is NOT a
sales call. Instead, we'll help you get a fresh perspective on your
business by allowing you to step back and see your situation with
fresh eyes. You'll walk away from this call with new insights
about what's working in your business and what you need to
address. We think you'll find this experience valuable whether or
not you choose to work with StrongLead in the future.

You can also download our free 7-minute People Analyzer to get
a quick and accurate snapshot of the ways that people are
contributing to your success and how they might be getting in

the way. In every business, regardless of size, people provide both fuel and frustration. This tool will give you a clearer picture of what's taking place in your business so you can determine how to move forward.

However you decide to move forward, we hope that you will continue to spend regular time growing as a leader. Remember, you're not just doing this for yourself, but you're doing this to benefit your team, your organization, and everyone you come into contact with. When the leader grows, everyone benefits.

Thanks for going with us on this journey. We wish the best for you in life and leadership, and we can't wait to witness the success you'll experience and the impact you'll have.

About the Author

Chad Hall serves as an Executive Partner with StrongLead. Chad has over thirty years of experience in leadership and working with leaders. His early career was in church ministry as a pastor, denominational leader, and seminary faculty. He also served as an internal coach with SAS in Cary, NC. His education includes degrees from Lenoir-Rhyne University (B.A.), Duke University (M.T.S.), Princeton Seminary (Th.M.), and Western Seminary (D.Min.). He also earned the designation of Master Certified Coach from the International Coaching Federation.

Chad is the author of several journal articles and books on the topics of coaching and leadership, including Amazon best-sellers *The Coaching Mindset* and *Coach the Person, Not the Problem*. In addition to his role with StrongLead, Chad is a founder and President of Coach Approach Ministries and is a founding board member of The Catawba Valley Leadership Foundation. Chad lives in Hickory, NC.

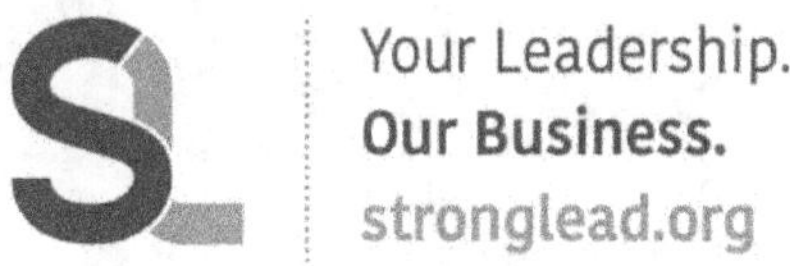

StrongLead is dedicated to strengthening the leaders who strengthen businesses, organizations, and entire communities.

www.stronglead.org

www.ingramcontent.com/pod-product-compliance
Lightning Source LLC
Chambersburg PA
CBHW070933260726
48661CB00003B/971

9798864017586